INTERIOR PRAYER

Other books in the Carthusian Novice Conferences series

The Way of Silent Love
The Call of Silent Love

INTERIOR PRAYER

CARTHUSIAN NOVICE CONFERENCES

by a Carthusian

Translated by
Sister Maureen Scrine

GRACEWING

First published in 1996 by Darton, Longman and Todd Ltd
This edition published 2006

Gracewing Publishing
2 Southern Avenue, Leominster
Herefordshire HR6 0QF

ISBN 0 85244 038 3
ISBN 978 0 85244 038 4

Printed in England

Contents

Acknowledgements

Grateful acknowledgement is given
to Sister Maureen Scrine
for her good-humoured patience and the
attentive quality of her translation from the French.
The essential contribution of the young monks for
and with whom the text was elaborated, and
of all who encouraged its publication is also
humbly acknowledged.

Introduction

The following conferences describe the gradual initiation of a group of young monks, over a period of about two years, into the practice of prayer. The approach is pedagogic; the style one of verbal exposition and discussion. The contribution of the novices at various points ('sharings') has been recorded as brief notes.

For these people, prayer is not just something that is done at certain times of the day; it is the vital respiration of their faith. The aim is continual prayer, that is all of life lived in conscious communion with God, life fully awake. This implies a certain vision of life, of humanity and of God, that is not developed theoretically here, but shown in its practical consequences.

Then, each of these novices describes his experience of prayer with its difficulties and lights. This is the starting-off point. To learn how to pray, Jesus by his example and his teaching is taken as a guide.

Certain forms of prayer, prayer of petition and intercession, are discussed. Finally, prayer in the name of Jesus brings together much of what has been said.

Prayer is a journey, sometimes a combat. There are trials, purifications, passages. It is at once the most simple and the most profound of human activities. May these pages help someone to discover its hidden joy.

The different forms that prayer takes as it unfolds from active to more contemplative into a life of prayer are then treated. More and more it is Christ who lives in the Christian and leads him into an ever deeper participation in the life of the Blessed Trinity. Union with God in this life is possible and the fulfilment of humankind.

Part 1

1

A Sharing on Prayer:
What is Prayer for Me?

Each of you is invited to speak of what prayer is for you not in theory, but at the level of experience.*

Peter
The first thing I would like to say, and, really, the only thing I have to say, is that I don't know what prayer is.

Here and now, that is what matters.

On an existential level, I am quite incapable of saying, after a time of prayer, whether or not I have really prayed. I just can't determine the dividing line between prayer and what is simply a rambling mind, or dreaming, or an emptiness which is only a completely natural rest or peace.

But that doesn't really worry me.

When you are actually praying, and you seem to be touching on real prayer, you think: this is it . . . or something quite different. Prayer itself is something you can't take hold of. Introspection can only touch on the psychological vehicle of it.

The different activities of mental prayer, reading, work . . . are not exactly what prayer is. I feel like saying that prayer is the heart. That doesn't make sense. I don't know how to express it.

There is a value in not knowing.

There's only one thing that matters: to believe or hope that the Lord is there at work in it, during or afterwards.

It's like a dish of mushrooms. There are the good ones and the bad. But how can you tell the difference?

---

*It is suggested that the reader before reading these accounts, or even afterwards, write down what prayer is for her or him concretely.

One thing is sure: you can't possess prayer; it's something interior.

What is prayer? Is it a gazing upon . . . ? I'm not completely happy with that expression. I would prefer a word that evokes a mutual gaze, God looking at me, and me looking at God.

I prefer 'presence', or 'abandonment' (but that doesn't say enough).

I used to be happy to say of time spent adoring the Blessed Sacrament, that it was just the fact of being there; like a sack of 'spuds', activity halted; distracted, but there.

What I want now is to let Christ pray in me. These are just words again, even if they do correspond to the theological reality. In real-life terms, I'm still searching.

I go to the oratory to pray. I don't know what I am going to. Afterwards, I don't know what I'm coming from. That's how it is at the moment.

James
I want to be concrete.

There's a great reality, a fact (though not obvious to everyone), God exists and he is our Saviour. He is a presence that we have to actualize.

1. On the one side: personal prayer.
    This can be represented by the words: listening, loving, being patient.
    To listen, that's the fundamental attitude; making oneself teachable.
    To pray is to try to let oneself be 'prayed'.
    The Word of God is a living reality, to be received, to let become flesh in me, to allow to come into contact with my personal experience, at the deepest possible level.
    To love: if it is real, prayer bears fruits of love.
    To be patient: from *pati*, to endure, to preserve . . . so as to be saved.
2. On the other side: liturgical prayer.
    It's a river, but made up of the streams that we are, if we are really cells of the Church, members of Christ.

But, on the subject of prayer in choir, I confess I have
reserves. The use of Latin, for example, is a question for
me. Where is the face of the Church in that? Latin is
marginal, though it may be helpful to some. The form that
prayer takes is important.

Being present to today's world. There's a link between
prayer and the widespread difficulty of coping with life. An
old ghost that was banished is coming back to life again:
God!

There are analogies and links between states of prayer and
the experience of psychoanalysis (infinite respect of the
person, birth to a truth that is deeper than self, the risks
of opening oneself up, etc.). A psychoanalytical experience
could well be the way towards a deep conversion. I don't
know why Christians are generally so suspicious with
regard to that. It could be seen as a divine answer to a
modern need. Real faith is not afraid of purification. The
face of God is too often hidden by the faces of our idols
and the concoctions of our ignorance.

But rather than talk about prayer, together let us now make a
practical experience of it:

(i)   we read slowly a few verses of the Scriptures;
(ii) we receive them in faith, letting them germinate in our
      hearts during a few moments of silence;
(iii) we let what seems the most beautiful word of what has
      been read rise in our hearts, we share it, pronounce it.

John

I don't quite know what prayer is. We are trying to talk about
our life in God, our degree of being.

We can distinguish specific acts of prayer, but all that we do
should be done in God; everything should be prayer. Ora et
labora: pray and work.

However, there are times that are more specifically consecrated to God, the Living One who gives us life.

Prayer is putting ourselves before God. It is exchanging a
mutual loving gaze (not thoughts). Being there, with, before

God. Doing nothing, not even speaking. Silence, letting oneself be loved, looked at, being receptivity. Welcoming, receiving everything, being there totally available.

Sometimes there is a dimension of intercession, a Church dimension. The prayer of the Office has priority over all other forms of prayer. It's the prayer of the Church, sure to be accepted by God. Grace makes us members of the Church, we have to be bearers of others, of our brothers.

One single Spirit unites us all. We must let the Spirit speak within us.

Having a right attitude before God is fundamental, otherwise we can't remain in his presence.

We are in the presence of the Father, as his sons in Christ, by the Spirit in our hearts: childhood, confidence, faith.

But we are also forgiven sinners: we are nothing. An attitude of humility is essential.

There is a sort of dialectic between the two attitudes: you have to hold both of them together.

My prayer is so poor, I haven't much to say –

- just being there, gratuitously, for nothing;
- trying to love: I don't know if I love, at least letting myself be loved;
- what exactly is praying? What matters is to go to it, even if it seems worthless. (At the end of the day, without prayer everything is a mess.)

Matthew

For me, prayer is something you can't take hold of: thoughts are different each day, the landscape changes; and yet, really, it is something very simple.

There are two parts:

    (1)   asking and receiving from God;
    (2)   giving thanks.

Sometimes the two exist together.

Prayer is the ability to be transparent. . . .

I think it is giving back to God what I receive. For example,

I look at a tree, and I offer it to him. Prayer is a current, and a state of awareness.

The more aware I am, the more I have to give.

The current is the Holy Spirit.

The Spirit is prayer, being transparent.

Being the instrument of the Father's glory.

The Spirit is a torrent, a spring that flows through me in proportion to my transparency, my purity.

Water, fire, to become one.

Being conscious of receiving, then offering to the Father, is transforming it into love.

I'm trying to express an intuition, it's not easy.

Prayer is the Spirit, and you can't understand the Spirit. The Spirit bears us away into the divine life. We don't possess the Spirit.

There is a kind of prayer that sets us on fire . . . A torrent that flows through us. Becoming fire.

Really, I only have one thing to say, to say to Him . . . You. Prayer is You.

Saying more seems superfluous to me, except perhaps to put different accents on it.

Arsenius

Prayer is your mystery. You, Father.

Your secret, Christ.

The magic of Love.

And Myself prayer, because You . . .

Prayer, it's this nothing, or this something without which nothing makes sense.

Perfect prayer, the Eucharist-Blessed-Sacrament, radiation of eternal love.

In the order of creation, which is prayer of God, the reflection of His prayer.

For me, the stars are the most beautiful symbol of this.

Prayer is sharing in, harmonizing with the immense, unique symphony.

Jacob

I don't know what prayer is either.

It is being in need at every level. On the day when the Holy Spirit descends, there will be no more prayer.

Prayer is an intermediate state.

My prayer is founded solely on faith in Jesus Christ.

I know neither the Spirit, nor the Father (except for a movement sometimes aroused in me).

I would like to spend long periods in prayer, but I'm incapable of it.

It's a relationship of trust with God.

My sense of the Church is not developed; at Office, in choir, I'm just doing my duty.

My prayer is a very personal thing. I don't have many thoughts about the Trinity, or Mary, or the Spirit.

I'm a blockhead. I have the impression of giving rather than receiving.

I'm not very intelligent, and won't amount to much.

I don't fight distractions, that's how I am.

My good desires are rotten at the roots, because I haven't the strength to do anything whatsoever.

I would like to spend a long time in prayer, be quite still, like one of the little crosses in the cemetery. Like an old dog . . . Like a little fly continually knocking against the window pane, sure that, one day, someone will open it.

The hours of Office, the psalms, all that is boring, it kills the Spirit. It would be better just to say 'thank you'.

Someone else's comment: I remember the story of the old peasant, in the time of the Curé d'Ars, who spent long moments at the back of the church, looking at the Blessed Sacrament. One day someone asked him: 'What are you doing during all this time?' . . . 'I don't say anything. I look at him and he looks at me.'

Comment: Right, but they don't say what he was doing before that; not rushing around!

Another comment: Night Office is like chewing-gum that you're ruminating.

Patrick

My prayer is listening to the other. What else can I say?

Prayer is above all a relationship of intimacy, of love; and so a two-way relationship.

Relationship to God first, but not exclusively. In the prayer of the Church relationships are multiplied.

It is a very deep sentiment that can't be shared, that can't be communicated; it belongs to the one who has it.

Prayer is that human space where you meet the other, with all you have, and have not.

There are many ways of expressing it; and every means of expression is good: vocal, verbal, instrumental, etc.

When you love, you listen: the one who is praying, just as much as the one who receives the prayer.

It's an exchange between God and someone who has not enough in himself, who is looking for something else, another himself; who is looking for himself.

There has to be a very deep sentiment of love.

Prayer is a sentiment of the heart. You can pray in joy or in suffering.

It is a relationship of love; that is all it is to begin with; a sentiment that transforms everything, to the extent of transcending absolutely all else.

It is a drive, that can be expressed in a look, in a gesture; it's a drive of love.

Like a child going to its parents with simple love that has nothing intellectual about it. He comes as he is – maimed, dirty, or whatever – with love, and simplicity, and detachment. That is how we can abandon ourselves to the other, to the Completely-Other . . . In the search for another self.

Everyone's prayer is different, depending on what is felt.

The quality of our prayer is the quality of our love.

The relationship to the Holy Trinity is very beautiful, and above prayer; that's what we are tending towards.

The Novice-Master

I don't like talking about prayer. I've been expounding the
theory of prayer enough lately; so if you don't mind I'm only
going to add a few crumbs to your banquet now.
   What is prayer for me?

> Nothing.
> Nothing added to what is, to the real.
> It is its transparency, if you like, its being there.
> It's the poetry of what is real.
> My faith, my life.
>
> Silence in the depths of the word,
> seeing in the darkness,
> a peace, an abandonment,
> a beating heart,
> lungs that are breathing.
>
> Christ.
> Mystery of life and death.
> Absolute hope.

> Water, that
> quenches,
> washes,
> refreshes,
> reflects,
> incorporates the light.

> Something ordinary,
> useful, beautiful, joyous.
>
> Or tears,
> a cry.

> Blessing of what is,
> of the One who is.
>
> Father, saviour.

Springing up from interior emptiness,
source of eternal life.

Spirit-Love.

You.

Nothing.

From this mystery springs forth God, the universe,
myself . . .
  Gratuitously, eternally.
    Through love.
      Table, flower, star.
        Why do we need wings to accede to what is
        infinitely close?
          Time, eternity.
            You, me, the ant, the mountain,
            God, man,
              emerging for the first time,
              in prayer,
                everything is one.
                How to pray?
                I no longer know how to pray.
                Why light a candle in broad
                daylight?

INFORMAL DISCUSSION AMONG THE NOVICES

(1) We mustn't forget the importance of desire in love. The
intensity of desire; the heart, a dry, weary land, without
water.
    The starting-point is the grace of the act of faith: God
exists! Joy of the young bridegroom. Thanksgiving, praise –
that's primordial – then a calm resting in the Lord.

(2) The importance of the Eucharist. Prayer is something
beyond us. As with the Eucharist, you are submerged into
it. You can see the Mass as being the source of prayer;
the reality of intimate communion with Christ, and with

my brothers. It can be prolonged during the whole day, and everything can be 'eucharisted'. Eternal life is given, truly, here and now, beyond psychological experience, in faith. Just as prayer is.

The capitulum for None: 'Whatever you do in word or deed, do everything in the name of the Lord Jesus, giving thanks to God the Father through him.'

(3)   For the Fathers of the Desert, the hardest thing in the monastic life is prayer. It's difficult to persevere in prayer. It's something that's above us, and beyond us. Abraham didn't know where he was going. Prayer will be given by the Spirit, one day.

(4)   For the feast of Corpus Christi, I kept a vigil before the Blessed Sacrament – twenty-four hours. I was tired – wanting to sleep or needing to be re-centred on myself – but he, on the contrary, was there all the time; he continues eternally, he is always adoring the Father. Eucharist, he lets himself be shared.

(5)   For me, the magnet is an image of prayer. The magnet attracts the piece of metal, but on the level of your senses, you can't make out which is attracting which. Prayer is the magnetic field that is created in this way. The piece of metal is being drawn; it doesn't know by what, but it is in movement towards. In human beings there is consciousness of being drawn; there is a state of desire. On earth, there's still separation. In heaven, it will be complete union.

(6)   For me, prayer is eternal. I can see myself praying eternally, singing the praise of God, with the thousands upon thousands holding their palms in their hands . . . the holy people.

(7)   Our being and our prayer will be the same thing. We are our 'weight' of prayer.

(8)   We will all, at last, be Carthusians!

2

Father–Son: The Prayer
of Jesus according to St Luke

St Luke is the evangelist who speaks the most of prayer. In this chapter we are going to meditate on the texts in which he shows Jesus praying. Looking at them as a whole, there is immediately something very moving about them, and which is of particular interest to us, Carthusians. For Luke is an evangelist who is writing in order to help us to pray as Jesus prayed.

OVERALL VIEW

I invite you first to look at the general chart on page 15. Certain fundamental truths stand out immediately.

- The Father is at the centre of the whole movement of prayer. Everything stems from him.
- Prayer is a dialogue between the Father and the Son, an engendering in the Spirit; and this is true from the moment the Spirit descends at the baptism, when Jesus is confirmed in his identity as Son and receives his mission.
- Through the purification in the desert and the refusal of an earthly messianism, Jesus walks in obedience to the will of the Father.
- His ministry is sustained by prayer.
- Jesus is acknowledged as the Messiah, the peak of his ministry.
- The Transfiguration prepares Jesus for failure which is already on the way.
- The revelation of the intimacy which exists between the Father and the Son.

- The communication of this intimacy to his mankind.
- The combat that takes place in prayer to assume, in his flesh, the will of the Father.
- The complete poverty of the cross, forgiveness and love towards humankind, total abandon in the hands of the Father.
- The resurrection, response of the Father, final engendering of the Son in glory.

Prayer is the heart-beat of life, here of Life itself, and so of our own life too. Let us be silent, and pray.

Let us allow ourselves to be drawn into this extraordinary movement which comes from the Father, from the Father's love, to be revealed in the love-obedience of the Son. Engendered by the Spirit, and having intimate knowledge of the Father, the Son reveals the Father to us; in a movement of unlimited self-giving and faith, he bears our sinful, vulnerable humanity right into the bosom of the Father. And he is, for us, the Way. His prayer is our prayer, his Father is our Father, for us who are engendered as sons in Christ by the Spirit.

Let us now take a brief look at each one of these texts. There are seven passages – and this is probably not just a chance figure – in which St Luke mentions explicitly that Jesus prays; one of them recalls a prayer made by Jesus in the past, whereas in the others we have the words of Jesus as he is praying.

THE BAPTISM

Now when all the people were baptised, and when Jesus also had been baptised and was praying the heaven was opened, and the Holy Spirit descended upon him in bodily form like a dove. And a voice came from heaven, 'You are my Son; today I have begotten you'. (3:21, 22)

At the inauguration of his public mission, Jesus is in prayer, turned towards the Father, waiting. He has just taken part in the baptism of repentance given by John, which was an invitation to purification and humility: 'Those who humble themselves . . . '
It is then that the Spirit descends upon him, and from heaven

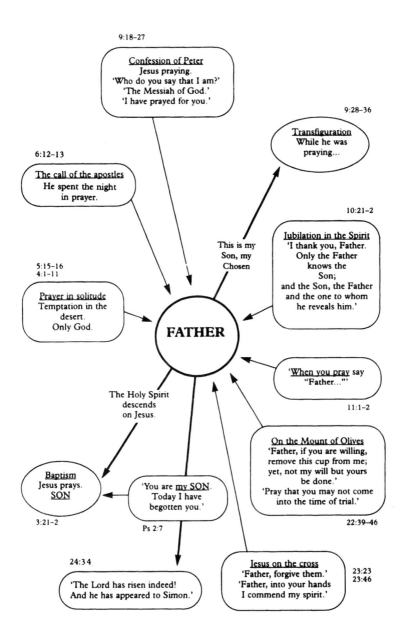

9:18–27

Confession of Peter
Jesus praying.
'Who do you say that I am?'
'The Messiah of God.'
'I have prayed for you.'

9:28–36

Transfiguration
While he was
praying...

6:12–13

The call of the apostles
He spent the night
in prayer.

10:21–2

This is my
Son, my
Chosen

Jubilation in the Spirit
'I thank you, Father.
Only the Father
knows the
Son;
and the Son, the Father
and the one to whom
he reveals him.'

5:15–16
4:1–11

Prayer in solitude
Temptation in the
desert.
Only God.

FATHER

'When you pray say
"Father..."'

11:1–2

The Holy Spirit
descends
on Jesus.

On the Mount of Olives
'Father, if you are willing,
remove this cup from me;
yet, not my will but yours
be done.'
'Pray that you may not come
into the time of trial.'

Baptism
Jesus prays.
SON

'You are my SON.
Today I have
begotten you.'

22:39–46

3:21–2

Ps 2:7

24:34

'The Lord has risen indeed!
And he has appeared to Simon.'

Jesus on the cross
'Father, forgive them.'
'Father, into your hands
I commend my spirit.'

23:23
23:46

the voice of the Father is heard: 'You are my Son, today I have
begotten you'. This verse from the psalm (2:7) signifies the
enthronement of the Messiah. Thus the Father manifests to
Jesus who he is, his fundamental identity as Son, and his
mission to the people of God as Messiah.

It is in humble prayer that he is given the light to know who
he is, the Son in the presence of his Father, and what the Father
wants of him; and it is in prayer that he receives the power of
the Spirit in order to bring his Sonship to fulfilment, in his
obedience to the Father.

The adventure has begun . . . Filled with the Holy Spirit, and
led by this same Spirit, he is, immediately after, to be tempted
by the devil in the desert for forty days. 'If you are the Son of
God . . . you must make the most of it! Make use of your spiritual powers in order to satisfy your hunger, to stun the crowds
with marvellous acts, to force your Father to manifest his love
for you . . . ' No!

- Man does not live by bread alone.
- Worship the Lord your God, and serve only him.
- Do not put the Lord your God to the test.

KING OR SERVANT

The temptation of a political messianism, of human success
brought about by human means, is present during the whole
of Jesus' mission. It will be a struggle for him to remain faithful
to the humble, hidden way traced out for him by obedience to
the Father's plan, a way that is infinitely paradoxical and senseless in the eyes of human wisdom. Jesus will reveal himself as
the Son in his fidelity not to appropriate the spiritual and
temporal treasures that are at his disposition. At the end of his
life, his love and his faith will be expressed in a poverty that is
total. But first of all, let us look at him at the time of his
'success'.

After a day spent preaching,

> More than ever the word about Jesus spread abroad; many
> crowds would gather to hear him and to be cured of their

diseases. But he would withdraw to deserted places and pray. (5:15–16)

Jesus has come into Galilee where he accomplishes healings. His fame has spread into the whole region. But Jesus has a deep desire: to withdraw into solitude to pray (4:42; see Mark 1:35). The crowd seeks him out again immediately, but he still has this desire for solitude, as is suggested in the order he gives to the leper he has healed: 'And he ordered him to tell no one' (5:14). There is a remarkable contrast between the solitude into which Jesus enters in order to pray, and the crowd avid to have words and healing from him, and ready to make him king in a completely political sense.

An incident recounted by Mark illustrates the same point. After feeding five thousand people in the desert, 'immediately he made his disciples get into the boat and go on ahead to the other side, to Bethsaida, while he dismissed the crowd. After saying farewell to them, he went up on the mountain to pray' (6:45–6). The miracle of the bread is a summit, and the peak of the political enthusiasm stirred up by the actions of Jesus. Moreover, the disciples share in this enthusiasm. Jesus refuses it. To effectuate this refusal, to lead this difficult choice to its conclusion, Jesus withdraws alone into the mountainside and prays. Only prayer, only the intimate and solitary contact with the Father, can enable him to stay at the level of his spiritual mission and to resist all the delusions of power.

THE CALL OF THE APOSTLES

Now during those days he went out to the mountain to pray; and he spent the night in prayer to God. And when day came, he called his disciples and chose twelve of them, whom he also named apostles. (6:12–13)

In order to open himself completely to divine light when it is time for him to call his disciples to share in his mission, Jesus spends the whole night in prayer; this is not the only time that Jesus prays during the night. And even then, one of the twelve

chosen will be 'Judas'. The hidden ways of God are such a
mystery!

PETER'S CONFESSION

Once when Jesus was praying alone with only the disciples
near him, he asked them, 'Who do the crowds say that I
am?' . . . and 'who do you say that I am?' Peter answered,
'The Messiah of God.'(9:18–22)

This is the turning-point in Jesus' ministry. He is acknowledged
as the Messiah by Peter; and Peter's faith can probably be
considered as linked to this prayer of Jesus: ' "Simon, Simon,
listen! Satan has demanded to sift all of you like wheat but I
have prayed for you that your own faith may not fail; and you,
when once you have turned back, strengthen your
brothers" '(22:31–2). Yes, the faith of the Church hangs on the
prayer of Jesus (John 17).

THE TRANSFIGURATION

Jesus took with him Peter and John and James, and went
up on the mountain to pray. And while he was praying,
the appearance of his face changed, and his clothes became
dazzling white. Suddenly they saw two men, Moses and
Elijah, talking to him. They appeared in glory and were
speaking of his departure, which he was about to
accomplish at Jerusalem . . . a cloud came and over-
shadowed them . . . Then from the cloud came a voice that
said, 'This is my Son, my Chosen; listen to him!'(9:28–36)

Jesus' star is already on the decline, and resistance to his
message is increasing. Once again, it is while he is praying that
Jesus is confirmed in his mission, which here is clearly that of
the 'suffering servant', to enable him to face the exodus he is
going to accomplish in Jerusalem. Behind the silhouette of the
cross, a little glimpse of the hidden glory of the resurrection
is given . . . in prayer. In advance, the faith of the apostles is
strengthened: 'This is my Son . . . I am his Father, and every-

thing is in my hands.' At this crucial moment, the revelation made at his baptism is repeated, made more clear.

THE HYMN OF JUBILATION

At that same hour Jesus rejoiced in the Holy Spirit and said, 'I thank you, Father, Lord of heaven and earth, because you have hidden these things from the wise and the intelligent and have revealed them to infants; yes, Father, for such was your gracious will. All things have been handed over to me by my Father; and no one knows who the Son is except the Father, or who the Father is except the Son and anyone to whom the Son chooses to reveal him.' (10:21–2)

When Jesus says that he is 'Son', he is affirming that he stands before God as a son before his father, accomplishing the work that he has been given to do, in complete and total accord with the will of the Father; trusting himself to him totally, living in his presence, having recourse to him each time he has to make a choice, speaking to him with the simplicity, the tenderness, and the security of a little child with his daddy (*abba*).

And God is Father for Jesus, in virtue of the way he acts towards him; because he leads him, hands his power over to him, confides his secrets and his plans to him, as a father does with his son.

There is a unique relation of intimacy between the Son and the Father, a total communion, in the Spirit, of their mutual love. It is within this relationship that Jesus is who he is; and it is in his prayer, above all, that his 'Sonship' is manifest. 'No one knows who the Son is except the Father.' 'Knowledge' is to be understood in the biblical sense of the word: a communion of love and of direct knowledge. Its source is in the gaze of choice and creation of the Father which rests upon Jesus, and makes him the Son. No one else can reach him at this depth. And no one knows who the Father is except the Son. To no one else has the Father revealed the mystery of his providence. No one else has acknowledged so profoundly the love of the Father, nor declared his fidelity with such a response of obedience, in which all his strength, his life itself, are consecrated to the accomplishment of the Father's plan. The Church is born of the participation in the knowledge of the Father communicated by Jesus to his disciples.

In a similar way, each of us, in Christ, receives a new name, a name written in the most secret recess of our heart, and known only to the Father. Sometimes, in prayer, the Spirit communicates to us in an ineffable cry (Romans 8) an incommunicable knowledge of the Father.

SAY 'FATHER'

He was praying in a certain place, and after he had finished, one of his disciples said to him, 'Lord, teach us to pray, as John taught his disciples.' He said to them, 'When you pray, say: Father . . . ' (11:1–2)

Jesus teaches prayer to his disciples by first praying in their presence. But at the same time he gives an example of what the content of this prayer should be. The first word, the essential word of Christian prayer, is 'Father'.

Say, 'Father'. We are, in all truth, his sons, sons by our faith in the Son, by the gift of his Spirit. Jesus has shown us how to behave as sons: to live in absolute trust of the Father, in obedience to his will of love, in the intimacy of solitary prayer, in the simple request of our needs, in the love of our brothers.

Father,
hallowed be your name;
your kingdom come.
Give us each day our daily bread.
And forgive us our sins,
for we ourselves forgive everyone indebted to us.
And do not bring us to the time of trial.

ON THE MOUNT OF OLIVES

He came out and went, as was his custom, to the Mount
of Olives; and the disciples followed him. When he reached
the place, he said to them, 'Pray that you may not come
into the time of trial.' Then he withdrew from them about
a stone's throw, knelt down, and prayed, 'Father, if you
are willing, remove this cup from me; yet, not my will but
yours be done.' Then an angel from heaven appeared to
him and gave him strength. In his anguish he prayed more
earnestly, and his sweat became like great drops of blood
falling down on the ground. When he got up from prayer,
he came to the disciples and found them sleeping because
of grief, and he said to them, 'Why are you sleeping? Get
up and pray that you may not come into the time of trial.'
(22:39–46)

At the centre of the narrative is Jesus' choice between his own
will, which expresses his human sensitivity, and the will of his
Father, which is the expression of his mission for the salvation
of humankind. It is a painful, tragical choice, and yet one which
is full of great dignity, and, finally, of great peace.

The narrative is presented in form of inclusion, within the
recommendation to pray so as not to enter into temptation;
and thus becomes a model of praying combat, supported by
strength from above.

The combat takes place during prayer. Jesus is intent on
communing with divine strength, seeking victory over his own
will. The mystery of God's infinite respect for human liberty,
and the vibrant reality of the humanity of Jesus are both
exposed, and most cruelly. What an encouragement for us in
our struggles between the will of God and the revolts of our
sensitivity!

JESUS ON THE CROSS

Jesus leaves this life praying. It is the moment of truth. Jesus'
truth in relationship to his brothers is forgiveness, the offering

of his life for those who are killing him; and in relationship to his Father, it is absolute trust.

'Father, forgive them; for they do not know what they are doing.' (23:34)

During his agony, it is not words of bitterness or revolt that come from his lips; not even a prayer for himself, for relief in his sufferings. All he asks for is the forgiveness of his torturers. 'Love your enemies, pray for those who persecute you.'

'Father, into your hands I commend my spirit.' (23:46)

In Luke's version, we do not have the cry of dereliction (Psalm 22:2; Mark 15:34), but a word of total abandon into the hands of the One in whom he trusts right to the end. The addition of 'Father' to the verse of Psalm 31:5 is highly significant. Prayer expresses the deepest movement of the heart; the heart of Jesus is totally turned towards the Father in the unity of his Sonship. His last words, as his first, express his love for the Father, 'Did you not know that I must be in my Father's house?' (2:49) But it is the Father who has the very last word. Having entered completely into the Father, Jesus becomes Life, and Source of the Spirit of Life. The glory of the resurrection is the Father's eternal response: 'You are my Son; today I have begotten you' (3:22).

THE STATIONS OF OUR PRAYER

One day the Father looked upon us, and chose us to be his sons. His Spirit came down upon us, and made us aware of our deepest identity; he whispered a secret name, and a way to follow. He drew us into the desert, to intimacy with him, and to a purification of our understanding of the coming of his Kingdom. We were confident in our human means; we had to learn the paradoxical ways of God, and poverty in the Spirit. Prayer in the night.

One day, the Church 'acknowledged' our vocation, and gave confirmation of our calling. She anointed us. We have been carried by the faith of the Church, and, supporting her faith,

by the prayer of Jesus. And our prayer, in turn, once it has
been purified, becomes a source for the Church, but a very
hidden source.

There have perhaps been moments of transfiguration, with
fleeting glimpses of the splendours of faith, to fortify us on our
way. Now it is past noon, and we are walking in greater light
towards death, yes, but more essentially towards the Father.

There are times of jubilation in the Spirit, when we are aware
of the unfailing goodness of God. Prayer is woven within a
trustful intimacy with the Father. As sons, obedient to his will,
we know him in a way that is utterly personal. And he knows
us. What peace there is in being known and loved beyond what
we know and love of ourselves.

As for us, let us try to communicate to our brothers, in our
conduct at least, the face of the Father.

Sometimes it is a combat. The perspectives of faith are lofty,
and how sensitive is the flesh of the human beings we are, how
lacking in courage. In prayer we draw strength to follow Christ
along the hidden paths of the Father. With Mary we say: yes,
Lord. Your will, not mine.

Then one day, there is the cross. At least, at the hour of our
death, the hour of our truth as sons, as human beings. Let us
pray that the face that we will then turn towards our brothers
may be a face of love and forgiveness. Let us start today!
And may the face that we turn towards the Father be one of
complete and trusting abandon, in the liberty of a love at last
released from its weight of earth and sin.

3

The Teaching of Jesus on Prayer according to St Luke

When we read the teaching of Jesus on prayer in St Luke's Gospel, we discover something very simple, and very beautiful. We are going to open ourselves to the texts in a spirit of prayer, as though Christ himself was speaking to us, with a minimum of commentary. It is the Word of God.

We will group the texts into four sections:

A. The heart of the one who is praying
B. The One we are praying to
C. How should we pray?
D. What we must pray for

A. THE HEART OF THE ONE WHO IS PRAYING

Only Christ, in his person, and through his Word, can reveal to us the face of God to whom we address our prayer. All prayer presupposes a welcoming of the Word of the Lord, and a heart enlightened by faith.

> 'Your eye is the lamp of your body. If your eye is healthy, your whole body is full of light; but if it is not healthy, your body is full of darkness. Therefore consider whether the light in you is not darkness.' (11:34–6)

The eye which enables us to see supernaturally is faith. By faith we can contemplate God's plan, the hidden meaning of things, insofar as our sight is not darkened by incredulity. The body probably means here the place in which the light has to live, the concrete aspects of our lives.

The one who hears the Word and obeys it (11:28), is enlightened by it in the whole of his existence (11:36). Only a heart that is pure and at peace can welcome the Word . . . so let us open up a space of silence to receive it.

'Sell your possessions and give alms . . . for where your treasure is, there your heart will be also.' (12:34)

'Give for alms those things that are within; and see, everything will be clean for you.' (11:41)

But detachment from the things of the earth is not enough. If the heart is neat and tidy, but empty, seven other spirits, more evil than the one which has been expelled, risk entering in, and 'the last state of that person is worse than the first' (11:26). So what danger we solitaries are exposed to if our hearts are empty of love! If I don't have love, I am nothing, my prayer is nothing! This is why it is so important to remain turned towards God's face of Love, so that our heart too should burn with love. 'There is need of only one thing. Mary has chosen the better part, which will not be taken away from her' (10:42). However true it may be that many services have to be provided, it is even more true that listening to the Word of the Lord is something unique which nothing else can replace (Acts 6:2).

Martha serves, and this is good. Mary's gift to the Lord is that she allows him to give; she gives her poverty and her love. That is the essential, the one thing necessary in God's sight, the only thing that is eternal. Through the ages contemplatives have seen in this incident an image of gratuitous prayer: a prayer that asks for nothing, but is exclusively occupied with the person of the Lord, intent on receiving the communication he is making of himself in his Word, receiving it into the depths of a heart that is open, silent, and attentive.

The 'better part' reminds us of the Levites' 'part' in the Old Testament cult (Deuteronomy 10:9; Joshua 18:7; Psalm 16:5-6). The new cult is to listen to the Word, in every home where there is someone to receive it. At root, prayer is sacerdotal.

But let us not oppose contemplative and active life. Every

Christian life has something of each of them, but in varying proportions. In St Luke, the passage about Martha and Mary forms a diptych with the Samaritan's act of mercy (10:25–37).

The Word of God winds its way secretly into the concrete of our lives, and sometimes it is the stranger and the heretic who are the first to find it, whilst the one who possesses the law of God (the priest, and the Levite) misses out on the profound inspiration of it, the mercy of God, and fails to manifest it in his actions. They have not recognised the Son, or the Father.

So in order to pray, the heart must be pure, animated with a deep faith, free from attachments to this world, and attentive to the person of the Lord and to his Word. What is it then that Christ tells us about the God to whom we are praying?

B. THE ONE WE ARE PRAYING TO

Jesus makes his disciples understand how they should address God by showing them what God's sentiments are with regard to them. It is above all as Father that Jesus speaks of God, and our behaviour is to be the practical consequence of what he tells us about him.

He, God, is good!

'Bless those who curse you, pray for those who abuse you . . . Then you will be children of the Most High; for he is good to the ungrateful and the wicked.' (6:28, 35)

Just as the Most High is good to the wicked, so we too must be good, to the point of loving our enemies and praying for them.

Jesus has rather surprising images as he tries to make us understand the goodness of the Father.

A goodness that is greater than that of the importuned judge

'In a certain city there was a judge who neither feared God nor had respect for people. In that city there was a widow who kept coming to him and saying, "Grant me justice against my opponent." For a while he refused; but later he said to himself, "Though I have no fear of God and no respect for anyone, yet because this widow keeps bothering me, I will grant her justice, so that she may not wear me out by continually coming."' (18:1–5)

If a wicked human judge is capable of acceding to the request of an obstinate, tiresome widow, how much more will not God, who is good even to the wicked, grant justice to his elect? And so it is that we must 'pray always and not lose heart' (18:1). We will certainly be heard; in the end God will answer our prayers.

Verses 7 and 8 give this lesson all its eschatological dimension. The 'days of the Son of man' will come most certainly (17:20–37).

A goodness that is greater than that of the importuned friend

'Suppose one of you has a friend, and you go to him at midnight and say to him, "Friend, lend me three loaves of bread; for a friend of mine has arrived, and I have nothing to set before him." And he answers from within, "Do not bother me; the door has already been locked, and my children are with me in bed; I cannot get up and give you anything." I tell you, even though he will not get up and give him anything because he is his friend, at least because of his persistence he will get up and give him whatever he needs.' (11:5–3)

Put yourself in his shoes! And conclude, a priori, from what you yourself would do, that that is what God does too.

A goodness that is greater than that of a human father

'Is there anyone among you who, if your child asks for a fish, will give a snake instead of a fish? Or if the child asks for an egg, will give a scorpion? If you then, who are evil, know how to give good gifts to your children, how much

more will the heavenly Father give the Holy Spirit to those
who ask him!' (11:11–13)

In Matthew, Jesus concludes by saying that 'the Father will give
good things to those who ask him.' Luke specifies, 'the Father
will give the Holy Spirit', the best of all the good things for
which the Church could ask. Prayer and the gift of the Spirit are
closely linked in the apostolic community, and in the Church of
all times.

The father of the prodigal son

One of the most moving images of the Father's goodness is the
father of the prodigal son. The poor lad, at last coming back
to his senses, decides to go to his father and to say to him:
'Father, I have sinned against heaven and before you; I am no
longer worthy to be called your son; treat me like one of your
hired hands.' But when he comes before the father, what a
welcome! 'While he was still far off, his father saw him and was
filled with compassion; he ran and put his arms around him
and kissed him.' He does not even let him finish what he is
asking, but interrupts him, saying to his servants:

> 'Quickly, bring out a robe – the best one – and put it on
> him; put a ring on his finger and sandals on his feet. And
> get the fatted calf and kill it, and let us eat and celebrate;
> for this son of mine was dead and is alive again; he was
> lost and is found!' (15:11–32)

This is the Father to whom we address our prayers, this is the
welcome we can be sure to receive, even when we come before
him as sinners.

4

'When You Pray'

C. HOW SHOULD WE PRAY?

Confident perseverance

Once we have understood that God is disposed towards us as a father, confident perseverance in prayer is a natural consequence.

> 'Ask, and it will be given you; search, and you will find; knock, and the door will be opened for you. For everyone who asks receives, and everyone who searches finds, and for everyone who knocks, the door will be opened.' (11:9–10)

The one who gives and opens is God. Ask, search, knock. Ask for everything, ask for the Spirit, seek God, knock at the door of the Kingdom ('Lord, open to us,' 13:25–7). Knock at the door which is Christ, he who is the way to the Father; through his wounds we have access to the Father, who, the first, is seeking after us in his Son. 'Listen! I am standing at the door, knocking; if you hear my voice and open the door, I will come to you and eat with you, and you with me' (Revelation 3:20). So when I pray, my prayer is only an echo of God's prayer. In that case, how could he refuse, refuse himself? What a mystery prayer is.

But my prayer has to be animated by the right dispositions, especially humility.

The humility of empty hands: the Pharisee and the publican (18:9–19)

The practical point made here is that the confidence we are to have in prayer must not be founded on our own 'righteousness', but solely on the merciful goodness of God, a foundation which is infinitely more secure.

We can read the parable in the present tense. The Pharisee and the publican are each one of us. The Pharisee boasts about his fidelity to the prescriptions of the Law, he even thanks God for what he is. This is good in itself, but instead of being consistent, and attributing to God the righteousness that he thinks he can see in himself, he takes it back as his own, and makes it an object of personal pride. He is neither a beggar, nor a 'useless servant'. He is full of himself. His scornful attitude towards his brother is the inevitable fruit of this.

As for the publican, he simply asks God to forgive him, for he knows he is a sinner. His attitude is simple. He is someone fulfilling his religious duties; to what extent, we don't know, but he goes up to the Temple to pray, just like the Pharisee. But he does not present God with his good actions, he does not calculate. He simply knows that he is a sinner, but that the Father is good; he commits himself to the mercy of God. This attitude obtains forgiveness for him, whereas the Pharisee remains imprisoned in the blindness of his own 'righteousness'. 'For all who exalt themselves will be humbled, but all who humble themselves will be exalted' (18:14).

Humility puts its trust in God alone. Behind this simple parable are the vertiginous depths of the doctrine of salvation by faith alone, regardless of merits. The only source of our certitude is the goodness, the gratuitous love of the Father, it is on that alone that we rely. 'What have we, that we have not received?' But what liberty in this radical poverty! – To live, as sons, in complete reliance on the infinite goodness of the eternal Father.

No bargaining

> He entered the Temple and began to drive out those who were selling things there; and he said, 'It is written, My house shall be a house of prayer; but you have made it a den of robbers.' (19:45–6)

In the Temple, God alone is to be adored. The man-made

dwelling place of the Old Testament is replaced by the Body of
Christ. We are this Body, the Temple of the Spirit. Only the
Spirit knows how to pray as we should. He cries out in us:
'Father'. He is Love.

Our heart has to be a house of prayer, a place where the Son
turns towards the Father in Love. It must be a place of silence.
The shouting of the traders has to be silenced! And the noise
of an even more subtle kind of bargaining, that of an attitude
that is too self-interested, woven of *do ut des*, of calculations,
and self-seeking. Beware of idols!

> **'And the Lord whom you seek
> will suddenly come to his Temple.'**
> (Malachi 3:1)

Vigilance

> 'Be on guard so that your hearts are not weighed down
> . . . with the worries of this life, and that day catch you
> unexpectedly . . . Be alert at all times, praying that you may
> have the strength to escape all these things that will take
> place, and to stand before the Son of man.' (21:34–6)

At the start of his public mission Jesus was tempted by the
devil for forty days in the desert (4:2ff.). Defeated, the tempter
withdrew from him (4:13). This defeat was repeated at each of
the exorcisms carried out by Jesus. But in God's plan, Satan
had his hour, the hour of the final temptation, the hour of the
Passion. Then he 'entered into Judas, one of the twelve' (22:3),
and succeeded in bringing about the death of Jesus.

Now the disciples too entered into a period of combat. It
had been predicted by Jesus. 'They will arrest you and persecute
you . . . By your endurance you will gain your souls' (21:12–19).

The Gospel evokes the eschatological temptation, the temptation of the last days, in terrifying, apocalyptical terms: hate,
death, anguish, pseudo-messiahs, and cosmic chaos. 'The
powers of the heavens will be shaken' before the coming of the
Son of man 'with power and great glory' (21:26–7).

The Church has never, in fact, been lacking in sufferings,

and is certainly not without them today. There is no return of
Christ, he has not shown himself, and remains invisible; he
does not answer our prayers or our desire (17:22). So we start
to doubt, we no longer have faith, we despair of God (18:8).
Why? Because we have to wait in faith until the very last day.
Or else it seems that our prayers are not changing anything;
and some of us tend to become drowsy, and to live carelessly,
exactly as happened on the eve of the flood and before the
destruction of Sodom; they were eating and drinking, buying
and selling, planting and building (17:28).

But there will be a sudden intervention of God, in the world
and in the lives of each of us. 'There will be two women
grinding meal together; one will be taken and the other left'
(17:36). 'Simon, Simon, listen! Satan has demanded to sift all
of you like wheat' (22:31). Every one of us is to be sifted like
wheat. Everything in us that is only straw will fly away in the
wind; only the grain will remain, that is, if anything remains at
all. Our faith itself will be sifted, even perhaps to the point of
falling away.

Will the Christian, the solitary, who feels the weight of the
absence of God, the long silence of the Lord, this Lord to whom
he is supposed to be speaking, persevere in really believing? Is
it not one of our temptations to sink secretly, almost uncon-
sciously, into despair, whilst continuing to live in a body – in
quite a reasonable one, but one that is empty of a soul, one
in which the practices and 'beliefs' of what is merely an ideo-
logical structure are devoid of value; where there is no real
expectation that this will change anything at all in a world in
which we are installed at ground level, quite a refined ground,
perhaps, but nothing more. As for the irruption of the Other
in this closed system, we are too polite, too 'humble', to think
that this concerns us personally.

Fortunately Christ has prayed for us (22:32). His prayer
awakes in us a faith in which we pray so as 'not to come into
the time of trial' (22:40, 46), just as Jesus himself prayed in his
agony of anguish on the Mount of Olives. He has taught us to
ask, in the Pater: 'Lead us not into temptation' nor to the
tempter, there behind the temptation.

Christ is with us, and we are with our brothers.

All those who have a role of pastor in the Church, and Peter, the first, are to strengthen the faith of their brothers (22:32). But this is also true, in the communion of the Church, of every Christian whose faith has come victoriously through a time of testing.

D. WHAT WE SHOULD PRAY FOR

Pray the Lord of the harvest (10:1-11)
When he sent the seventy-two disciples out to preach, Jesus gave them two orders: to pray, and to proclaim that 'the Kingdom of God has come near to you' (10:9). 'Ask the Lord of the harvest to send out labourers into his harvest', for 'the harvest is plentiful but the labourers are few' (10:2).

It is in prayer that the apostolic Church chooses and sends her apostles, praying to obtain for them the power of the Spirit. This was the case on the very first day of the evangelization of the world: the disciples in prayer received the gift of the Spirit and began to proclaim the marvels of God. The proclamation of the gospel is a work of the Spirit; its efficacy comes from the power of the Spirit. That is why Jesus asks us to pray to God that he may send his labourers. Unless God gives the grace of the Spirit, all human efforts and initiatives, however sincere they may be, are vain and useless. It is God who gives the increase, God alone.

This is why the Church relies so much on the prayer of contemplative men and women as a necessary complement, as the soul of the activity of her apostles. The patroness of missions is a young Carmelite nun, who never left her cloister, but whose love and prayer travelled all over the world.

The harvest represents the eschatological judgement of the world, a judgement which has already begun in the acceptance or the refusal of the Word which announces the presence of the Kingdom of God. This is the drama of every day, the eternal drama.

Jesus raises his eyes over the immensity of the world (John

4:35), and sees that everywhere the field is waiting for the harvester. Everywhere there are spirits seeking the light, eyes looking out for salvation which is hoped for, but unknown, hearts crying out their thirst for true justice and true love. In contemplation, these things are presented to our own eyes, and we continue Jesus' cry to the Father: 'Thy kingdom come'.

Strive for the Kingdom, and these things will be given to you as well

'Do not worry about your life . . . do not keep striving for what you are to eat and what you are to drink, and do not keep worrying . . . For it is the nations of the world that strive after all these things, and your Father knows that you need them. Instead, strive for his kingdom, and these things will be given to you as well. Do not be afraid, little flock, for it is your Father's good pleasure to give you the kingdom.' (12:22, 30–2)

The word 'search' is part of the vocabulary of prayer in the New Testament: 'Ask, and it will be given you; search, and you will find' (11:9). Jesus teaches us to have a certain indifference with regard to material cares that are a constant preoccupation in the world. Not that we too do not need to eat, and be clothed, and receive a certain education, and be in a secure environment, especially on an affective level: all the basic requirements that are needed simply to make a human life possible. But, even on this level, there is so much we can quite well do without: so many artificial needs created by the publicity of a consumer society, greedy for profit and money, and with an unquenchable lust for pleasure. We do have needs, but the Father knows them much better than we ourselves do; he has nothing to learn from us on this. The Father loves us, we who are his sons and daughters; and his providence governs all things. If we ask for our daily bread, it is because the Lord wants us to do so, and has taught us to do so, teaching us in this way how poor and dependent we are.

But we pray with calm and confidence, respecting the scale of values. The essential is the Kingdom. We must ask for the coming of the Kingdom, and that is what we must seek before all else. The rest will be added on for us as well. We can abandon the cares of these secondary needs so as to be completely intent on the Kingdom. This is what our vocation is all about. It is easy to see what the content of our prayer must be. In any case, the Lord does not leave any ambiguity about this.

Our Father

'When you pray, say:
Father, hallowed be your name.
Your kingdom come.
Give us each day our daily bread.
And forgive us our sins,
for we ourselves forgive everyone indebted to us.
And do not bring us to the time of trial.'

(11:2–4)

'Father'. I, your son, say to you, God: 'Father'. Proximity, confidence, simplicity. You know me. I know you. I try to accomplish the task that you give me to do in my life in perfect and total accordance with your will.

'Hallowed be your name.' 'Make yourself acknowledged as God' (French ecumenical translation of the Bible). Your Name designates your being. It is holy above all else. We can add nothing to your holiness, but we can acknowledge it for what it is, and glorify it. Men and women of all times, and especially the people of Israel, have tried to sanctify and glorify your Name, by obeying your commandments and by acknowledging your Majesty in prayer of pure praise, both in community and personally. But, on the one hand, they were not able to be holy as you are holy, and to obey your commandments, and on the other, the knowledge they had of you was obscure, and only a distant reflection of your true splendour.

So it was that there arose from Israel, and from the pagans too, a fervent prayer towards you, to sanctify you and glorify you, by manifesting you as Saviour in the eyes of all humankind. But you alone can establish your reign among us, you alone can reveal yourself in your power and your glory, in your justice and your grace.

'Your Kingdom come.'

Your answer is your Son, his person, his life and his death. You have shown us the secret of your being, the gratuitous, merciful, overflowing Love of a Father for his sons. You have drawn us to yourself as if with two arms, your Son and your Spirit. The Spirit poured out into our hearts, has made us your sons in Christ, able to cry out 'Father' in total confidence; to ask that the holiness of your Love, your real face, be known to all humankind; that your reign of justice, forgiveness and peace be established in the hearts of all, and in the whole human community. You alone can accomplish that; but you want us to be associated in that task by commanding us to ask it of you in our prayer, by making our hearts into openings, breaches, through which your grace can enter into the world and flow out among our brothers, as it flowed out through the wounds of your Son hanging on the cross.

For it is by the weakness of Love that you want to establish your Kingdom. Your infinite power is a power of real compassion that knows no limits, of forgiveness that does not draw back, however great an evil human beings may inflict upon themselves, it is communion of life offered in pure gratuity, dependent on nothing other than your infinite Goodness.

You wanted to respect human liberty, and allow history to unfold in time: but in a time which has meaning and direction since it is moving towards the plenitude of your reign in the total-Christ, through a slow, obscure gestation. May our prayer hasten your coming, Lord. Maranatha!

And because we are beings of flesh, with our needs, taking daily sustenance from your creation, we ask you, Father, in all simplicity, for the bread that we need each day. You know well what our needs are, we trust you, and have no worries.

And then, Father, forgive us our sins. Forgive us for not always acting as your sons, for not acting as you do. Forgive us, Father. Receiving life from your forgiveness, we too forgive all those who have wronged us. It is not always easy, Father, we are so sensitive and bitter, but how else can our hearts be open to receive your forgiveness? We would be hypocrites, and in your presence, Father, nothing is hidden.

For this very reason, because you know our weakness, do not expose us to be tested above our strength. Guard us from entering into the tempter's views, from colluding with him, and 'falling into temptation' (1 Timothy 6:9).

Father, we know that we can always count on you.

5

The Prayer of Petition

The prayer of petition is regarded as something quite normal in the Old and New Testament. It was both practised and taught by Jesus himself. In the history of the Church there has only been one heresy that has contested it. In the seventeenth century, the Quietists affirmed that when a person comes to the perfection of Christian life he no longer feels the need, and no longer has the right to ask anything of God: such a prayer of petition was to be considered as a rebellion against the inflexible will of God.

However, we have to admit that prayer of petition is questioned by many of our contemporaries. Why?

Recourse to God is not encouraged by the modern mentality. People find it hard to believe that God can or wants to help us in our real problems. Prayer, they say, weakens our determination to solve our problems, by ourselves. It is regarded as a 'substitute action', which is more or less a capitulation, and a pernicious and ineffective one at that.

Besides this, doesn't the prayer of petition imply a false image of God? If, in the prayer of petition, I am in any way expecting something from God, inevitably I must be imagining him to be like a king, with special powers at his disposition: and by prayer, I am trying to make him act in the way I want. God would be a sort of 'kindly God', obliging and easily influenced, rather arbitrary and changeable. Moreover, how can we envisage 'exceptions' in the necessary laws of the cosmos?

But, above all, and most importantly, is not God true, completely unfathomable, transcendent, unchanging and eternal? In short, for many of our contemporaries, meditation, yes, is acceptable; but not the prayer of petition. But meditation, as an effort of concentration, a gathering together of all one's energies in order to arrive at control of oneself and of the world, is not specific to the Christian faith. This can also be learnt, and even better perhaps, from the masters of meditation in the East. No, we cannot get round the problem so easily. Prayer of petition is an integral part of our vocation. But often, perhaps, our understanding of it is too superficial.

There are, in fact, two questions:

1. Can prayer, of itself, be objectively efficacious, that is, can it change anything in the exterior ordering of the world?
2. Why is one prayer answered, and another not? (But we will look at this question in another conference.)

Here, let us try to answer the first question. On a metaphysical level:

CAN PRAYER BE OBJECTIVELY EFFICACIOUS?

Historically, this question seems to be a direct consequence of the development of philosophical reflection and the technical mentality. These both rest upon the same basic presumption of the necessity of the material world, and they are characteristic of the modern mind.

For the primitive mentality prayer flows spontaneously: the gods are close, and made of the same stuff as human beings, the material world, the stars; everything is one. Prayer flows as it were naturally in a world where the necessities of life are continuously bathed in the sacred, and where the considerably flexible benevolence of the gods at the service of men and women is not questioned.

With the coming of the Western mentality, all this is changed. The Greeks impose the idea of a world ruled by necessity. In the domain of religion, this takes the form of a Destiny weighing down upon both human beings and gods. In the sphere of eternity nothing can change. Everything is fixed with regard to eternity.

In the scientific field, all science is founded on the idea of a constant, universal law, that of a necessity which rules the world we experience. The whole of our technical civilization is based on determinism. So, in this universe of empirical forces, the knowledge of which enables human beings to act with certitude, it is quite unthinkable to introduce an energy of another kind – prayer – of which the efficacy can only be conceived in terms of liberty, and so of unpredictability.

In order to get round this objection, the temptation is to limit the field which can be influenced by prayer, excluding every effect which could be objectively examined, and leaving only the moral and spiritual area. This would lead us to accept only those forms of prayer which are perfectly disinterested: thanksgiving and contemplation. Prayer would then be left only with a pedagogue function. Renan, for example, did not deny that there is a certain value in the prayer of faith: 'But I can only give it a subjective, psychological value', he said. 'It is a way of edifying and comforting one's own self. But it would be superstitious to expect it to produce any objective result, for everything in the world is subject to the necessities of the laws of nature.' As for Freud, he affirms that even the psychic phenomena of our feelings and desires are ruled by determinism. In his opinion, the explanation of the efficacy of prayer is to be found in natural causes of a psychic order: illusion, autosuggestion, the action of the subconscious self on the 'spiritual universe' (a vast collective subconscious) etc. These efforts to find an explanation obviously fall short of the facts of experience, where we find objective answers to prayer, which can be verified in the material world.

So we are faced with two big questions:

- how cosmic determinism relates to the liberty of God;
- and how prayer relates to the accomplishment of the eternal will of God.

COSMIC DETERMINISM AND THE LIBERTY
OF GOD

Both positivists and determinists want to be rational and scientific.

In spite of appearances, and although such positions are

free from the popular anthropomorphisms of the primitive
mentality and the Bible, they are not untouched by a more
subtle form of anthropomorphism. The eternal necessity
which they affirm is hardly more than the projection into
the absolute of the idea of a cosmic necessity conceived
by the human intelligence, based on experience: that is to
say, a necessity which excludes free decisions, and their
unpredictability. But the power of God the Creator is
something completely different! Not only does it imply a
wisdom which brings everything into existence 'with
measure, weight and number' (Wisdom 11:20), but also
the will of the Creator to maintain the universe throughout
time, a will which is capable of englobing every kind of
activity on the part of the creature without violating human
decisions in any way: and this with regard to the liberty of
spirits just as much as to the determinism of laws.

On a deeper level, someone who prays looks less to the structure
of the world than to its finality. In the end, it doesn't really
matter if events take place in accordance with necessary, known
laws, or because of some unpredictable intervention of God.
What is important is that the believer should be able to acknowledge that the loving will of the Father disposes all things in
view of his good. The one who prays does not ignore the order
of natural laws; but his view of the ordering of the world differs
completely from that of the determinist. For the former, this
order is not a rigid succession of phenomena, following on in
uniform manner, like the links of a chain. Rather, it is a living
organism in which countless forces unite, interweave, and react
with one another, and in which all can contribute to a finality
freely willed by God: the glory of God and the good of
humanity. A whole vision of the world is implicated in prayer.

And at the same time, in its most far-reaching research,
particularly in the domain of micro-nuclears and macro-
phenomena (astrophysics), science itself has already gone
beyond a too simplistic determinist vision of the universe.
Matter is more mysterious than was thought, and the laws we
can perceive in it are not absolute, they are only 'static': which

means that they are the expression of what *usually* seems to happen on a particular level of existence, but not absolutely always; there is a margin of indetermination, or 'chance', which they do not control. The idea of some free causality, such as prayer, becoming a part of the universe of causes, is no longer unthinkable.

But let us examine this from the point of view of God.

PRAYER AND THE WILL OF GOD

In the Gospel prayer is presented as indispensable, and as having an effect upon the will of God – 'Ask and it will be given you'. As we have seen, persevering prayer is shown there to be efficacious, almost, it might be said, unconditionally (Luke 11).

This doctrine came through in an even bolder way in the Old Testament. When, for example, Moses was interceding for the rebellious people which had made itself a golden calf: 'Turn from your fierce wrath; change your mind and do not bring disaster on your people. Remember Abraham, Isaac, and Israel, your servants . . . ' (Exodus 32:12–13), the answer is astonishing: 'And the Lord changed his mind about the disaster that he had planned to bring on his people.' So for us who live in time, prayer has a before and an after, just as there is a before and an after in the reception of a sacrament. How can the efficacy of prayer be expressed more clearly than by saying that it changes God's plans? 'The prayer of the righteous is powerful and effective' (James 5:16).

There are many other examples to be found in the prophets. Among the saints, it suffices to quote St John Climacus: 'Prayer does holy violence to God'; and St Jerome: 'The prayers of the saints can resist the wrath of God'.

And yet the God we are praying to is the Father 'with whom there is no variation or shadow due to change' (James 1:17). His word is all-powerful and absolutely effective (Isaiah 55:11). God's designs are eternal and cannot in any way depend on the prayer of his creature for their accomplishment.

We know that believers were sensitive to this difficulty,

through the witness of Origen who, in the fourth century, expressed thus the objection of a correspondent: 'Firstly, if God can foresee the future, and this future will surely come to pass, then prayer is useless. Secondly, if everything happens in accordance with the will of God, and if his designs are stable, if he cannot change anything of what he wills, then prayer is useless.' How can we reconcile statements which seem to be so contradictory?

The solution is that it is not only the effects which appear in the cosmos, and in human history, that God wills: he also wills their causes, the totality of their causes, those that are determined by the laws of physics and those that depend on human liberty, which includes prayer. By a free disposition of divine providence, prayer has its place in the order of causes, and produces effects that are eternally willed by God. How great then is the responsibility of all those who are called to a service of prayer.

The difficulty comes from the fact that practically the only way we have of imagining the relationship between the world and the knowledge and will of God is in the form of two energies working towards the same end. In this case, the amount of energy attributed to one is subtracted from the other. We have to replace this image of two rival forces situated on the same level, by one that is less inadequate. We have to think of the whole of creation, the order of nature and the order of liberty, as englobed in a vaster sphere: that of an all-powerfulness which transcends the different created modes of action. Or, put in another way, the whole order of time is contained in eternity. It is not sublimated, in such a way as to be extinguished; on the contrary, it is confirmed in its reality of temporal succession. By maintaining the world in existence, divine action confirms it in its continuity. So, for us who live in time, and who can only think in terms of time, the efficacy of prayer has to be expressed in terms of time. So, once again: there is a before and an after in prayer, an irreversible succession between the request made and the answer given. The whole of Scripture, which is a sacred history and a progressive initiation into the true knowledge of the living God, must be seen in this perspective, which alone can justify prayer.*

It is with this depth of meaning that we can interpret a text of St Thomas, which gives all its value to a reflection of St Gregory:

> It must be remembered that not only the effects produced are a part of the dispositions of divine Providence, but also the causes, and the way in which they are brought about. And human acts must also be counted among these causes. So various actions have to be accomplished by men, not in order to change the divine dispositions by their acts, but that by these acts they may bring about effects in accordance with the disposition of God's plan.

This is true both of natural causes and of prayer. For we do not pray in order to change the divine dispositions; but so that God may accord that which, in his plan, is to be accomplished by the means of the prayers of his saints. That is to say, in order that 'mankind, by their prayers, may merit to receive that which almighty God has decided from all eternity to give them', as St Gregory says in the book of *Dialogues*. To be properly understood, such statements have to be viewed from a contemplative standpoint. Only then can we see all things englobed in the sphere of the knowledge and the eternal love of God: the laws which rule over the world, as well as the effects expected and the co-operation of human beings – that of their prayer.†

SUMMARY

We can draw a certain understanding of the prayer of petition from these difficult philosophical considerations.

---

*C. Bernard, *La Prière Chrétienne*, p. 142.
†S.T. 2.2., Q. 83., A 2. The whole of Q. 83 of the *Summa Theologica* of St Thomas can be read with profit.

The world is not a machine, a mechanism in which every movement is determined, but a place of life, that has come from a living intelligence, and is impregnated by it, open to the action of God. and borne by a finality of love. In this world in which we live, the effects of prayer are objective and can be verified.

Prayer is the work of God

Prayer is a gift of God. From all eternity God has wanted this prayer that I am making here and now, at this point in time, in view of a particular effect, which he has also willed from all eternity.

And yet I make this prayer freely; on my part, it is an act of faith and love that is meritorious. And it is freely that God answers my prayer.

God, by his grace, by the action of his Spirit, inspires me to pray. I pray. God answers my prayer.

'Why did God create prayer? In order to bestow the dignity of causality upon his creatures' (Pascal): real causality, placed between an initiative of God and his fulfilment of it.

God in his mercy has freely decreed that it is only with the collaboration of humanity that he will accomplish his plan of salvation: and prayer is an example of this.

6

The Efficacy of Prayer

Why is one prayer answered and another not? Tradition has often asked this question in the following way: what conditions are needed for a prayer to be *efficacious*?

The answer given was: '*necessaria ad salutem, pro se, pie, perseveranter.*' 'Things necessary for salvation, for oneself': there we have the object of the prayer; and 'with piety and perseverance' – this is how the prayer is to be made.

FOR WHOM SHOULD WE PRAY?

Is the only efficacious prayer then the one we make for ourself? Of course not! When tradition affirms this, it simply means that when I ask something for myself, that very prayer expresses my desire, and disposes my heart to receive the object of my prayer; whereas, when I pray for someone else, I have no assurance that this person will be open to receive it.

When I pray for others, my prayer comes up against the same limits as the love of God: the liberty of others. God, all-powerful as he is, does not force the liberty of others, and neither does prayer, which can be held in check by it. When I pray for a sinner, this sinner can say no to the grace of conversion which, thanks to my prayer, is offered to him. Our prayer shares in the mystery of Christ's redemption: a mystery of infinite love, which, however, remains powerless in the face of refusal by a human liberty.

This painful incertitude must encourage us to pray all the more insistently for our brothers. We know how profoundly grace and liberty are linked. It may be that my prayer will be just the little grain of sand that tips the scales. In any case, I cannot stop knocking at the door, in the certitude of sharing in the prayer of the Church, which is taken up into the sacrifice of Christ. As far as we are concerned, let us try to assume this fully in the prayers of intercession that are placed on our lips during Divine Office and the celebration of the Eucharist.

For us monks, prayer for others is a sacred duty of charity, and something that we owe in justice to the poor who are our brothers (St Thomas speaks of 'spiritual alms'; I would rather say 'justice'), which, paradoxically, we have a duty to give, precisely to the extent in which we are poor. But conscious of a mystery that is beyond us, let us pray with great humility, without calling the Lord to account.

THE THINGS NECESSARY FOR SALVATION

The ultimate object of our prayer, as of our desire, must always be eternal life, union with God; there can be no other object that is worthy unless it is subordinated to this end, both for ourselves and for others. In this way, our will is totally conformed to the will of God, who wants our salvation. But salvation, and the Kingdom of God, are mysterious realities, and very often the ideas we have of them are so petty.

> May God have mercy on you, and may he not allow your spirit to find firm ground on which to rest! And so, my soul, in spite of yourself, you will come back to the Ark, like Noah's dove.*

In practical terms, we ask to acquire some particular virtue, to obtain some special gift, or to be spared a suffering, or other such things . . . that we see as being for our own spiritual good, or for the good of our neighbour. But the answer to our prayer may well be: 'My grace is sufficient for you, for my power is made perfect in weakness' (2 Corinthians 12:9). In God's plan, this infirmity is for our good. Perhaps the way of Love, for us, is to be the way of poverty and of the cross.

If I ask for what is necessary for salvation, my prayer will always be answered. If I ask for what seems to me to be neces-

---

*Guiges, *Thoughts*, 340.

sary for salvation, my prayer will be answered as to its substance, but not necessarily in line with its explicit content. So our prayers must always be made under the reserve 'if this really is in accordance with your will, in accordance with your Love'.

We do not always know how to ask for that which is God's will for us, but the Holy Spirit knows. The Spirit within us rectifies our requests by inspiring us to ask for the right things.

> The Spirit helps us in our weakness; for we do not know how to pray as we ought, but that very Spirit intercedes with sighs too deep for words. And God, who searches the heart, knows what is the mind of the Spirit, because the Spirit intercedes for the saints according to the will of God. (Romans 8:26–7)

HOW WE SHOULD PRAY: WITH PIETY

If our prayer is to be answered, it must be an expression of the right attitude in the presence of God. And this attitude is revealed to us by Christ, he who, 'in the days of his flesh, offered up prayers and supplications, with loud cries and tears, to the one who was able to save him from death, and he was heard because of his piety' (Hebrews 5:7).

(The Jerusalem Bible notes: the term 'piety' implies respect and submission, and what we call the 'virtue of religion'. The prayer of Jesus during his agony was still inspired by total obedience to the will of his Father. This is why he was heard and answered.)

Our own prayer must be full of the same dispositions as those that are in Christ Jesus:

- the love of a son for his Father;
- absolute trust: I believe in You;
- concrete hope in his loving, all-powerful providence which watches over all things: 'the very hairs of your head are numbered';
- humility which acknowledges one's fundamental poverty:

'the prayer of the humble pierces the clouds' (Sirach 35, 21);
- love of one's neighbour: the Father does not hear the prayer of a heart from which his son is excluded (Matthew 5:23);
- unswerving obedience to the Father's will, even in the sacrifices he asks of us for the realisation of his Kingdom;
- in a word, the purity of heart that seeks only the glory of God.

This is 'praying in the name of Jesus', and we know that 'the Father will give you whatever you ask him in my name' (John 15:16).

So we understand the ardent efforts of the first monks to obtain purity of heart. And we understand too that we cannot obtain it by our own efforts alone. It can only be a gift of God, grace, 'the love of God poured out into our hearts by his Spirit'. Our effort consists entirely in removing the obstacles, so that the prayer-love of Christ himself can spring from the depths of our heart, in all its purity and in all its breadth, to embrace the whole of humankind.

This is where acts of penance have their place, fasting, and mortifications, to support our prayer (Matthew 17:21), and make reparation; to restore an order that has been disrupted by sin (our own sin, or the sin of those for whom we are praying). In this way, prayer becomes something more total, that engages our whole person, and takes on a greater existential weight.

WITH PERSEVERANCE

Jesus often insists on this: we are to pray with perseverance and not to be discouraged, if God does not give an immediate answer. He will most surely hear our prayer. In practical terms, we must have courage, and know how to endure in prayer.

One day Abraham, the disciple of Abba Sisoes, was tempted by the devil. And the old man saw that he had given in. Rising up, he stretched out his hands to heaven saying: 'God, whether you like it or not, I won't leave you until you have healed him.' And immediately the brother was healed.

But here again, the facts of experience force us to probe deeper. Take the case of a sick person who has been to Lourdes several times, and who has not been cured. We have already seen that things we ask for are not always for our spiritual benefit. But how infinitely wise God is. By the virtue of our persevering prayer, if the Lord does not answer us according to the desires of our own will, there will be a gradual harmonising of our own will with what the Lord desires. This is what happened during the prayer of Jesus in Gethsemane. Prayer gives us a better understanding and acceptance of the situation, and makes us see with God's eyes. What begins as a request for healing, can gradually become, through patience, a life offered in reparation.

PRAYER AND ABANDON

The prayer of petition can lead us to a spiritual attitude in which our deepest desire is realised in a radical transcendence.* Taking into account how difficult it is to know exactly, at every moment, what God's will is, it is possible for someone to come quite simply to the point of surrendering themselves to his good pleasure, and abandoning all preoccupation as to what they should desire and ask for. They leave it to God to decide what is best, and to give what is needed at the right time. They become an unconditional 'yes' to the will of God, in all that he asks for or allows. As for them, they ask nothing, except to grow in love; and they refuse nothing, except sin. 'All things work together for good for those who love God' (Romans 8:28). This of course requires considerable spiritual maturity. Mary is the perfect model of this.

On the other hand, the prayer of petition will never be absent, in the form of intercession for others, and for the Church.

---

*'When it is God's will that we should desire something, and we, on our side, abandon ourselves to his will, we are, in fact, asking him for that which will come from the help we await from him.' (S.T. Sent).

Abandon calls for intercession, just as the love of God calls for love of our neighbour.

But, faced with the petitions of our prayers, the Lord always remains free, and capable of intervening when he wishes, and in the way he wishes. This is the unfathomable mystery of his wisdom and of his eternal love.

In fact, prayer will always prove to be the mystery of two liberties, one of which knows that it is eternally enfolded in the love of the other.

> O the depth of the riches and wisdom and knowledge of God! How unsearchable are his judgements and how inscrutable his ways ... For from him and through him and to him are all things. To him be the glory forever! Amen. (Romans 11:33–6)

THE PRAYER OF STARETZ SILOUAN

The soul that is filled with the love and humility of Christ weeps and prays for the whole world.

If you will pray for your enemies, peace will come to you. 'The enemy persecutes our Holy Church', you may say. 'Am I then to love him?' But my answer is this: 'Your poor soul has not come to know God, and how greatly he loves us, and how longingly he looks for all men to repent and be saved. The Lord is Love, and he sent the Holy Spirit on earth, who teaches the soul to love her enemies and pray for them that they too may find salvation. That is true love.'

Some say that monks should serve the world, so as not to be eating bread that they have not earned. But what does the service of a monk consist in, how is he to help the world? Well, the monk prays with tears for the whole world, and that is his principal task. And what is it that drives him to pray and weep for the whole world? In the Holy Spirit, Jesus, the Son of God, gives the monk love: and his soul is in continual anguish for humanity for many are not seeking the salvation of their souls.

I have no other wish but to pray for others as I do for myself. Praying for others means: *giving the blood of one's own heart.*

When the soul prays for the world, she knows better without newspapers how the whole earth is afflicted and what people's needs are. Prayer cleanses the mind and gives it a better vision of all things.

Thanks to monks, prayer is unceasing upon the earth, and that is how they are useful to humanity. The world holds together thanks to prayer. If prayer stopped, the world would perish.

O Lord, give to us this love throughout thine whole universe! O Holy Spirit, live in our souls, that with one accord we may all glorify the Creator, Father, Son and Holy Spirit! Amen! Amen! Amen! Alleluia!

Turn to God, all you peoples of the earth, and address your prayers to him. If the prayer of the whole world ascends to him, in a great, silent column, then all the heavens will exult and sing the praises of the Lord, for his passion which has saved us.

7

The Prayer of Intercession

The people of the land have practised extortion and committed robbery; they have oppressed the poor and the needy, and have extorted from the alien without redress. And I sought for anyone among them who would repair the wall and stand in the breach before me on behalf of the land, so that I would not destroy it; but I found no one. Therefore I have poured out my indignation upon them . . . I have returned their conduct upon their heads. (Ezekiel 22:29–31)

The prayer of intercession is a form of the prayer of petition, in which we pray for others. The one who is interceding is praying to God in order to obtain some particular benefit for his fellow human beings: a benefit that is always related, more or less directly, to the spiritual aim of his or their union with God. In order to fulfil his role, the intercessor has to be in contact with God by a living faith, and with his brothers by sincere charity, so that he himself becomes as it were a conductor wire, through which the divine power of salvation can pass to reach his brothers.

It is one of the aspects of our monastic vocation that, in Christ, and through the Spirit, we are transmitters of the life and love of God to our brothers, especially to those who are separated by sin from the source of life. In Christ, and moved by his love, we are chosen to be mediators of the divine life by our whole life and especially by our prayer. The liturgy is constantly putting on our lips a magnificent expression of this prayer of intercession, but it is up to us to animate this prayer with genuine love and a deep faith.

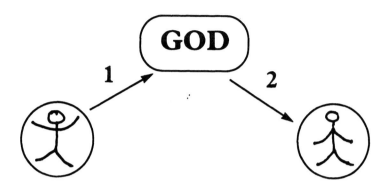

Why then does God want this prayer of intercession, how do we pray in this way, and what is it for?

As we have seen, God does not want to save us without our co-operation. He gives us the dignity of taking part with him in the realisation of his plan of salvation: Christ, first of all, and then us, in the power of his Spirit. Apostolic activity and the witness of a truly Christian life are forms of this co-operation. And so is prayer.

By prayer we exercise causality in the spiritual order. Superficially, we could think of it as making pressure on God, who then acts upon the beneficiary of our intercession.

We have seen that the reality is not quite so simple. Prayer of intercession is the work of God. Right at the beginning is an initiative of God, inscribed in the eternal decrees of his providence. God sends his Spirit, who inspires in the heart of the intercessor the desire to pray for a particular intention, perhaps because of some exterior event. This prayer rises to God, and, to the extent in which the beneficiary is open to receive his grace, God answers it; and this grace will always have the effect, more or less directly, of an increase of divine life in the beneficiary. In the prayer of intercession, essentially, a current of divine life passes through us to our brothers: a life of knowledge and love of God and of our brothers. It is the mind of God and the love of God communicated by the Spirit of God.

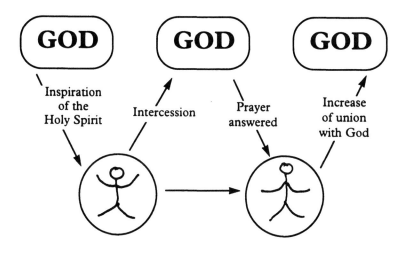

It may be that, at first, we do not experience the inspiration of the Spirit as such, but simply as a desire to pray for a particular intention, out of compassion for some human distress. On our side, the requisite is a radical capacity to receive this movement of the Spirit (and this is the work of the gifts of the Spirit), and a very great docility to his promptings. Prayer is first of all receptivity to God's action. The conditions of this receptivity are the attentiveness of a listening ear, and the purity of a heart in which no obstacle or resistance is to be found. This docility and state of receptivity are not to be limited by our capacity to understand. The ways of the Lord are not our ways. Through us, it is God who is appealing to the beneficiary of our prayer.

Once the request is made, it is God alone, in the end, who sees to its accomplishment; even though it may not be easy for us to understand the means he chooses to attain his ends.

We can see better what prayer really is if we look at it from the interior. The inspiration of the Holy Spirit, and his grace, are not airy-fairy things: they take flesh in our human spiritual activity, in our thoughts and desires. Our heart is filled with the sentiments of God towards a particular person or group of persons: sentiments of mercy, compassion and love, which contain the saving, healing power of God. And these thoughts and sentiments do not remain enclosed in our own hearts, but go directly to the beneficiary of our prayer. How does this happen?

To understand, we have to reflect a moment on our human condition. We are spirit-bodies. Our bodies are very precisely circumscribed, within limits of time and space. But our minds are not. Our interior life, our thoughts and feelings, do not remain within the borders of our body. They come out of it, as it were, and spread out into the living milieu of the whole of humanity, into the biosphere which is made up of the inter-action of all the spiritual forces that permeate our milieu.

In prayer, the Spirit communicates something of the life of God to me, something of his thoughts and of his love. This live current runs through my human activity to reach the person I am praying for, and brings him perhaps that very grace of healing or faith for which I asked. To communicate it to him, God inspired that prayer in me, and used my heart as a con-ductor wire. We can see analogies of this in the natural order.

At this very moment innumerable waves are crossing this room: waves of light and sound, and all sorts of electromagnetic waves. I am not aware of most of them, because I have not the adequate capacity for receiving them. But if we switch on a radio, the room will be filled with music coming from Paris, Berlin, Dublin. There are also more subtle 'waves' crossing the room, those which constitute the psychic 'atmosphere' of the place. There are 'waves' emanating from each of us, which can be felt by others, more or less distinctly, depending on their sensitivity. Under their influence they can either feel comfort-able, or, on the contrary, have an unpleasant impression. We can say of a group, for example, that the atmosphere is 'charged' or 'relaxed', depending on the sentiments of the people in the group, be they aggressive or anxious, or, on the contrary, well-disposed. These are sentiments that are communicated inevi-tably, even in the absence of word or gesture. (Those familiar with the 'Vittoz' method know that a live current, of love or peace, for example, can be deliberately directed towards a particular person. This can be useful in choir sometimes!)

There is another, more intimate way in which the Spirit communicates himself to our brothers, and which is generally from within the invisible communication of the deep spiritual attitudes of our heart that we have just mentioned. Here, to the degree in which we are transparent to his action, his Love passes through our love, and his solicitude passes through ours. This communication is not limited to those with whom we have some sort of contact, as in the case of psychic waves (the extent of which is already difficult enough to determine): it moves freely in the spiritual universe. It is limited only by the strength or weakness of our love and our faith.

Our human environment is also traversed by spiritual influences coming from God, or the angels; and from evil spirits too.

Each of us can be likened to a transmitter, sending out 'waves' at various levels; and, in the same way, each one of us is under the influence of all sorts of other waves, as a receiving post.

So you can see the importance of the spiritual quality of our innermost thoughts and feelings. If they are positive, we are sending a current of Life into our human environment; if they are negative, we are polluting it with a poisonous current. (The flow of influences, so often harmful, which pour down on our contemporaries through television, radio, cinema, and publications of all kinds, is an image of this transfer of invisible spiritual influences.)

We can assume that someone who is open to God in contemplation, letting the light and love of God enter into his heart, without concerning himself directly with intercession, reaches the same result: the light and the love that are received are communicated into the spiritual environment, and can benefit this or that person in particular in a secret and hidden way. In this sense, every thought that is in accordance with God, every movement of the heart in accordance with Christ, is prayer. And every thought that is contrary to love, every negative movement of the heart, contributes to the work of evil in

the world. The realisation of this truth is quite terrifying. It
is the whole of our interior life projected onto a television
screen in front of everyone. 'Beware of hypocrisy . . . Nothing
is covered up that will not be uncovered, and nothing secret
that will not become known' (Luke 12:1–2).

In practice, we behave generally as if it is only what we
express in our exterior acts that matters. And yet the teaching
of the Gospel is formal. In all his teaching, Jesus emphasises
the importance of the dispositions of the heart, for example:
'Out of the abundance of the heart the mouth speaks' (Matthew
12:34); 'Out of the heart come evil intentions, murder,
adultery, fornication, theft, false witness, slander. These are
what defile a person' (Matthew 15:19–20).

We are called to be 'transformed by the renewing of our
minds' (Romans 12:2). We have to 'take every thought captive
to obey Christ' (2 Corinthians 10:5).

8

Transmitters of God

Let the wicked forsake their way,
and the unrighteous their thoughts;
let them return to the Lord,
that he may have mercy on them,
and to our God, for he will abundantly pardon.
For my thoughts are not your thoughts,
nor are your ways my ways,
says the Lord.

(Isaiah 55:7–8)

In Christ we are called to be transmitter sets, transmitters of God, and to separate ourselves from all thoughts that are contrary to his thoughts, so as to transmit to others only the thoughts of God. This is a priestly function of great value with the task of interceding for the world.

The person we are is determined by what we usually think and feel. And it is from our heart that our behaviour proceeds. There is a struggle within us between good and evil, each trying to take over our spirit (Romans 7:14ss), unless we allow the Holy Spirit to take control of it. Our spiritual activity then expresses the life of God, his thoughts and his love. It is only then that the Kingdom of God becomes a reality within us. That is what the life of grace is, and salvation that is promised. To the extent that we are not saints, we are harmful to our brothers, we pollute the air they breathe. That is what it means to 'sadden the Holy Spirit'.

If we break off our contact of love with our brothers, by giving in to thoughts and feelings of hatred, anger, bitterness, resentment, jealousy, self-pity, and egotism, then however beautiful our prayers are, the contact is switched off, and we are no longer transmitters of God. Without love, we can no

more transmit the life of God than a radio can transmit anything
if it is not plugged in.

> If I speak in the tongues of mortals and of angels, but do
> not have love, I am a noisy gong or a clanging cymbal . . . if
> I do not have love, I am nothing. (1 Corinthians 13:1, 2)

As long as we harbour in our heart an attitude towards someone
which is contrary to love, that person will not be receptive to
our thoughts; on the contrary, our thoughts will attack him. It
will be useless to pray for him; in fact, it would be hypocrisy
to do so. But be careful: we are not talking here about superficial
reactions of sensitivity, but of profound, deliberate attitudes. If
we have the desire to forgive and to love a person whom, on
the level of our sensitivity, we do not like, the contact of charity
is in no way broken off, and our prayer for him can be effective.
The contact can only be broken when we willingly open ourselves to sentiments of hostility, and nurture and prolong them,
and not by feelings over which we have no control. So we have
to identify and immediately eliminate any antagonistic thoughts
towards our brother, as soon as they come into our minds.
Otherwise we are letting the forces of evil use our minds as
transmitters of hatred, anger, and evil.

Genuine intercession is founded on thoughts and desires that
are formed in us by the Lord, by Love. In this case, our heart
is a transmitter, sending out thoughts of mercy and healing, of
forgiveness, strength and creativity to the hearts of our brothers,
who receive them as promptings to open themselves up to light
and to life and to love.

Prayer is said to be a conversation with God; it is here that
God communicates something of his thoughts to us, something
of his light and his love. We are formed at the school of his
Word. In order to pray, we have to dwell in Christ.

God looks at the real desires in the depth of our hearts, even
though we ourselves are perhaps barely conscious of them, and
our words do not express them. It is when our human faculties
are moved by the Spirit, and become the lyre of the Spirit, that
they are the most fully themselves, it is then that they are
what they were created to be.

Now the works of the flesh are obvious: fornication, impurity, licentiousness, idolatry, sorcery, enmities, strife, jealousy, anger, quarrels, dissensions, factions, envy, drunkenness, carousing, and things like these. I am warning you, as I warned you before: those who do such things will not inherit the kingdom of God. By contrast, the fruit of the Spirit is love, joy, peace, patience, kindness, generosity, faithfulness, gentleness, and self-control. There is no law against such things ... If we live by the Spirit, let us also be guided by the Spirit. (Galatians 5:19–25)

To be transmitters of God's life, we have to purify our hearts: not just our exterior acts, but our thoughts and sentiments.

If you are angry with a brother or a sister, you will be liable to judgement. (Matthew 5:22)

Everyone who looks at a woman with lust has already committed adultery with her in his heart. (Matthew 5:28)

We are constantly transmitting sentiments and thoughts. Are they always according to God? Are they not sometimes those of the enemy? We let bad, worldly, impure influences find their way into us, through carelessness, and it is those waves that we then transmit.

Our struggle is not against enemies of blood and flesh, but against the rulers, against the authorities, against the cosmic powers of this present darkness, against the spiritual forces of evil in the heavenly places. (Ephesians 6:12)

We are both transmitters and receivers. It is what we first let enter into our hearts that determines the quality of what we transmit. So it is crucial for us to know how to distinguish between the good influences that come from the Holy Spirit, and the bad influences that come from the spirits of evil and from others. We have to protect ourselves actively against harmful influences that fill the atmosphere.

It is because the monks of old knew this so well that they were so exercised in the discernment of thoughts and inner purity of heart. For them, the word 'thought' did not mean an abstract idea, but something conceived by the mind, in concrete circumstances, and charged with emotions and desires. It is in this existential sense that we are going to use the word 'thought' in what follows.

The control of our thoughts by vigilance (*nepsis*) is absolutely necessary for a life of prayer. We have to cultivate the guard of the heart, a vigilant attentiveness to the thoughts which continually come into our minds, so as to welcome those that are good and exclude the bad ones. This is a hard discipline, but we have seen how important it is.

THE SERMON ON THE MOUNT

To help us, Jesus has carefully exposed for us in detail the eight spiritual attitudes that are beneficial, and the nine spiritual poisons. The former are the beatitudes, that make our souls healthy and happy to receive salvation.

- 'Happy' are those who are animated by the Spirit and the thoughts of Christ. Theirs is a deep joy that radiates around them.
- 'Blessed are the poor in spirit', those who are not filled with greedy desire for the things of this earth. Rather, they put their trust in God and live in filial dependence on him, receiving with joy all that his providence sends them. They are poor of themselves, and centred on Christ.
- 'Blessed are the meek'. Meekness is the opposite to violent self-affirmation. It is a spiritual attitude of a soul that endures everything, and forgives everything, with no grudges or resentment.
- 'Blessed are those who mourn', who bear the weight of the world's distress with sincere compassion; and who bear the weight of their own weakness and sin with an attitude of deep compunction, but without being crushed by it. They know that they are saved.
- 'Blessed are those who hunger and thirst for righteousness', those who want to establish the justice of love in their

thoughts, words and acts, and in human society. It is an attitude that is always open to more light.

- 'Blessed are the merciful', those who neither judge nor condemn their brothers' failings, but who welcome them in their weakness and pour the oil of charity over their wounds.

- 'Blessed are the pure in heart', those who are transparent to the will of God, because in the depths of their heart they are unreservedly open to the love of God and of their brothers.

- 'Blessed are the peacemakers', those who are factors of unity and reconciliation, and who do not sow seeds of discord and hatred.

- 'Blessed are those who are persecuted for righteousness' sake': those who, in Christ, accept with patience and forgiveness all that God allows others to do or say against them.

These are the attitudes of the children of God, led by the Spirit. They are the biosphere of the Kingdom of God, here on earth and in heaven.

The opposite attitudes are what hell is made of, here on earth and in the next world. These are diseases of the soul, the fruits of sin. Jesus clearly pointed them out in the same sermon, in chapters 5 and 6 of St Matthew's Gospel. I will just outline them:

- 'Woe' to those in whom the thoughts of evil dwell. They are filled with sadness and give out waves of sadness.

- Thoughts of anger and scorn with regard to our brothers (5:21–6).

- Impure and licentious thoughts (5:27–32). They are so pernicious that our Lord tells us to oppose them vigorously: 'If your right eye causes you to sin, tear it out and throw it away' (v. 29).

- Unjust and deceitful thoughts (5:33–7). 'Let your word be "Yes, yes" or "No, no", anything more than this comes from the Evil One' (v. 37).

- Thoughts of retaliation and revenge: an eye for an eye (5:38–42).
- Thoughts of hatred and refusal to forgive (5:43–8). Even where our enemies are concerned, love heals and hatred poisons.
- Thoughts of vanity and self-admiration, showing off (6:1–18): the habit of comparing ourselves advantageously to our brothers, and lowering them in our thoughts whilst exalting ourselves. An inclination to delight in daydreams in which we are the glorious heroes of the endless films in the cinema of our imagination, which make us irritable and critical of others.
- Thoughts of covetousness and ambition (6:19–24). God or the possession of objects and honours.
- Thoughts of anxiety for the future (6:25–34). We are in the Father's hands. 'Do not worry about tomorrow, for tomorrow will bring worries of its own. Today's trouble is enough for today' (v. 34). We need a faith that is effective, committing us concretely to total dependence on God, when he is clearly calling us to some particular act.
- Thoughts of judgement and criticism of our brothers (7:1–5), the speck and the log. Turning over and over in our minds the weaknesses and faults and mistakes of others, under the pretext of praying for them, leads to exasperation and is the death of brotherly love.

  And these thoughts that are communicated, in a mysterious way, to our brothers, drive them more deeply into their problems, and bind them even more strongly. 'Whatever you bind on earth will be bound in heaven, and whatever you loose on earth will be loosed in heaven' (Matthew 18:18), (even in thought). How destructive our prayers are, when corroded by a spirit of judgement: instead of being creative, transmitting the thoughts of God, his 'faith' in human beings, and his forgiveness!

It is our soul, first, that is poisoned by all these thoughts; they may also have an effect on our body, and then throughout the biosphere of the spiritual world of humanity. Doctors and

THOUGHTS

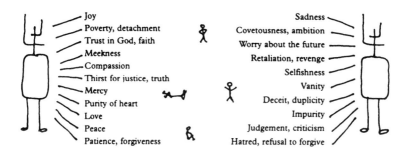

Joy
Poverty, detachment
Trust in God, faith
Meekness
Compassion
Thirst for justice, truth
Mercy
Purity of heart
Love
Peace
Patience, forgiveness

Sadness
Covetousness, ambition
Worry about the future
Retaliation, revenge
Selfishness
Vanity
Deceit, duplicity
Impurity
Judgement, criticism
Hatred, refusal to forgive

THE HUMAN ENVIRONMENT

psychologists are increasingly aware today of the effect that our thoughts have on our health and balance. Jesus has shown us which thoughts are beneficial, and which are harmful. It is, indeed, a terrible exigency; but within us we have the strength of the Spirit, we have Love. If we allow ourselves to be led by the Spirit, we will act as children of the Father.

We can conclude by saying that the Lord has taught us the perfect prayer, which expresses the desires of a purified heart, docile to the Spirit: Father . . . hallowed be thy name . . . thy kingdom come . . . thy will be done . . . give us our bread . . . forgive us . . . deliver us from evil.

THE GREAT FIGURES OF INTERCESSION

The reader is invited to select and meditate on one or the other of the great men and women of intercession in the Old Testament.

Abraham: the friend of God, who made a covenant with him; intercession for the sinners of Sodom: the righteous should not perish with the unjust (Genesis 18 and 19).

Jacob: wrestles with God in order to 'snatch' a blessing for himself and for the people born of him (Genesis 28:10–22; 32:23–33).

Moses: mediator of the Covenant at Sinai, and of God's Law, prophet, leader of the people; solidarity with the people always, for better and for worse. Profound experience of God, intimacy with him, bold intercession for the people (Exodus 14:15–31; 17:8–16; 32:9–14; 33:18–23; Deuteronomy 3:23–7; 4:22).

Jeremiah: intercession that comes from a tender heart, ravaged by the role to which God calls him (Jeremiah 14 and 15).

The Servant of the Lord: a mysterious figure, innocent; by his sufferings accepted in obedience, he bears the consequences of the people's sins and becomes a source of salvation for many. The redemptive value of suffering (Isaiah 42:1–4, 5–9; 49:1–6; 50:4–11; 52:13–53:12).

The Psalms: the poor of Yahweh.

The Kings and Priests of the Jewish people who pray for Israel and offer sacrifice to God (especially the High Priest in the liturgy of Kippur).

Mary: her 'yes' is totally open to the action of God, source of life for all.

Now, Jesus.

9

The Intercession of Jesus on Earth

JESUS THE MEDIATOR

The mediator is one who unites two elements that are separate. One of the dimensions of mediation is the prayer of intercession. Individuals who are pleasing to God place themselves in all openness before him, and, completely in solidarity with the people of sinners, try to obtain God's grace for them.

Basically, it is not a question of trying to make God change his mind. God is eternal and does not change. Rather, it is a means used by God to accomplish his will, his plan of mercy and salvation.

It is the grace of God that inspires the prayer in the heart of the one who intercedes; and the love which is at the source of this prayer is being communicated to him by the Spirit of God. That love is communicated to the one for whom he prays, and in this way God's plan for him is accomplished. The finality is always communion with God, eternal life. The prayer of intercession goes from God to God, and it is, in the last analysis, an act of our liberty adhering to God's plan of love.

Christ is the supreme mediator. He is so, first of all, *ontologically*. As the Word incarnate, he unites the divine nature and human nature in his own person, in a way that is absolutely unique. The divine and the human are united in a single person, without being either merged or separated (the hypostatic union).

As in every other human being, the humanity of Christ is an historical reality, which develops within the framework of time, subject to the laws of human growth, and following a personal history. In Jesus, his personal history is the existential expression of the ontological union of his two natures, human and divine. Prayer is an essential dimension of this, as an adhesion from the depths of his heart to his existence and to his mission.

The prayer of Jesus has its specific place in his human will. Its domain is the work that the Father has given him to do on earth: the establishment of his Kingdom in the world. This is the object of his ardent desire, and hope, and so also of his prayer; it is the prayer of his love, and of his whole life – and of the sacrifice of his life.

THE PRAYER OF JESUS ON EARTH

We can make a distinction between the prayer of Jesus on earth, and his prayer in heaven. (The prayer of Jesus in heaven, and his intercession as the risen Christ, are more especially treated in the letter to the Hebrews, and in the writings of St Paul.)

Jesus' prayer on earth, the prayer of his humanity, addressed to the Father, is described to us in the Synoptics as inseparable from all the most important moments of his life (the baptism, the temptation in the desert, the call of the apostles, the confession of Peter, the transfiguration, the Mount of Olives, and on the cross). At every step along the way of his mysterious destiny as the Servant, Jesus prays. He prays to the Father in simplicity and trust, sometimes with tears, always with love. He has taught us how to pray, and what to ask for: the coming of the Father's Kingdom, Our Father ... (We have already studied this when we looked at the prayer of Jesus in St Luke's Gospel.) We can complete this teaching with two passages from St Matthew which are particularly relevant here.

(a) Prayer in secret (Matthew 6:5–8)

In secret. Jesus wants our prayer to be pure, for God alone. Not the hypocritical ostentation of those who 'love to stand and pray in the synagogues and at the street corners, so that they may be seen by others' (v. 5). Seen by others, not by God. They have already received their reward.

'But whenever you pray, go into your room and shut the

door and pray to your Father who is in secret; and your
Father who sees in secret will reward you.' (v. 6)

In secret. 'Secret' implies something that is separated, set aside
(from the Latin *secernere*). A place apart. In solitude. In the
depths of the heart, beyond the sound of words (v. 7). In
silence. Alone with the Father, in the silence of the Father. For
the Father is there, in that secret place, he sees in secret.
Only the Father.

Note that the Gospels always show us Jesus on his own when
he is praying. In solitude, he can assume the meaning of his
own unique existence in the presence of the Father.

(b) Prayer in the communion of the Church
And yet:

> 'If two of you agree on earth about anything you ask, it
> will be done for you by my Father in heaven. For where
> two or three are gathered in my name, I am there among
> them.' (Matthew 18:19–20)

There is also a time for praying together, and for gathering
together as the Church. This is not an ordinary gathering, but
meeting together in the name of Jesus, a union that is operated
by the Word of Jesus and in his Spirit of love. Then Jesus is
there in the midst of us, and the Father will answer our prayer.

THE PRAYER OF JESUS ACCORDING TO ST JOHN

John's perspective is between heaven and earth, between time
and eternity. It is John who projects the light of Easter most
clearly onto the earthly Jesus. He shows us the prayer of Jesus
from the point of view of his divinity. From the beginning and
for always, Christ is the incarnate Word. He is the one who is
with the Father, from all eternity, the Word by which all was
created; the only Son, who alone knows the Father, and who
alone can reveal him.

John records only one real prayer of intercession of Jesus: the
great priestly prayer which expresses his whole mission and

the whole of his life. But this prayer, so exceptional, can only
be understood insomuch as we see it as an expression of the
intimate and constant communion which exists between Jesus
and his Father.

(a) Communion with the Father

Jesus lives in constant union with the Father. He is the Son,
who alone knows the Father (6:46). This filial relationship
constitutes his person.

It is in Jesus that heaven and earth mysteriously enter into
communication. John the Baptist sees 'the Spirit descending
from heaven like a dove, and remaining on him' (1:32). Jesus
himself takes up the image of Jacob's ladder: 'You will see
heaven opened and the angels of God ascending and
descending upon the Son of man' (1:51).

From now on, his body is the true Temple of God (2:21).
Jesus knows that he has been sent by the Father, and that he
has come down from heaven to bear witness to what he has
seen and heard. He speaks 'the words of God', who gives him
'the Spirit without measure' (3:31, 34). The Spirit is within
him 'living water . . . a spring of water gushing up to eternal
life' (4:14), that he will communicate to all those who thirst
(7:37–9), when his mission is accomplished. Jesus is the true
adorer in spirit and in truth that the Father seeks. He alone
knows the Father and can adore him in all truth, and with all
his being. His adoration is freed from dependency on times
and places (chapter 4).

His will is perfectly accorded to the will of the Father. 'My
food is to do the will of him who sent me and to complete his
work' (4:34). His eyes are constantly turned towards the Father.
'The Son can do nothing on his own, but only what he sees
the Father doing' (5:19).

Jesus does not seek the glory of human beings; he does not
seek to do his own will. That is why he speaks the truth:
he communicates the words of the Father; what he does is
accomplished through him by the Father.

The Father had given him power over the life of men and
women, and authority to execute judgement over them (5:30).

Jesus, the Living One, lives by the Father. The Father is always with him, and does not leave him alone, because he always does what is pleasing to him (8:29). No one can convict him of sin (8:46).

Jesus' union with the Father is more than the union of a holy man with God. Jesus can apply to himself the expression applied in the Old Testament to Yahweh, 'I am' – '*Ego eimi*' (8:24). He claims for himself the divine attribute of eternity: 'Before Abraham was, I am' (8:58). He affirms a unity with the Father that is more than simple union: 'The Father and I are one' (10:30); 'the Father is in me and I am in the Father' (10:38). Possessing, each of them, the same divine nature, the Father and the Son are 'one'; whilst remaining, face to face with one another, two distinct persons. Jesus' proximity to God is, then, infinitely greater than that of any other mediator, and that is why his confidence is so extraordinary: he knows that the Father always hears him (11:42).

(b) Distance

And yet there is also a distance between Jesus and the Father. Jesus is a real human being. The human sensitivity and capacity for human emotions of the Word incarnate is not suppressed by his proximity to God, but rendered more acute. We see him moved by sentiments of astonishment, friendship, sorrow, and fear. Faced with the inevitable suffering of the passion, his heart of flesh trembles.

> 'Now my soul is troubled. And what should I say – "Father, save me from this hour"? No, it is for this reason that I have come to this hour. Father, glorify your name.' (12:27–8)

There is a certain duality between the natural will of Jesus, on the level of his senses – a will which is, however, always conditional (if it is your will) – and his deliberate, absolute will (his attachment to the will of the Father). It is inside this duality that we have the presentiment of the mystery of his prayer, in all its pain: the tension towards a total 'yes' to God through the darkness of time and the weight of the flesh.

Truly human, Jesus is bound to the rest of humanity by every fibre of his being. Moreover, it is God's plan that all those who believe in him be incorporated into him, to form a single body, and as it were, a single person, the total Christ, of which Jesus of Nazareth is only the nucleus. John expresses this reality in the images of the Shepherd and the vine.* The Shepherd (ch. 10) knows his sheep, and is known and loved by them. They follow him. He gives his life for them, and gives them eternal life. In the parable of the vine (15:1–10) we can see an even deeper union. Christ is the vine itself, we are the branches. His life, the sap of eternal love, flows into all the branches. 'Those who abide in me and I in them bear much fruit, because apart from me you can do nothing' (v. 5).

Union with Jesus leads to union with the Father. 'On that day you will know that I am in my Father, and you in me, and I in you' (v. 20). On that day! The reality of perfect intercommunion is for the last days. The great prayer of Jesus, called the priestly prayer, is resplendent with the light of the resurrection; but it is also the expression, in the form of prayer, of the whole mission of the incarnate Word.

(c) The priestly prayer (17:1–26)

Let us try to enter interiorly, by the heart, into the movement of this prayer. It is not a problem to be resolved, but a mystery to be lived, a mystery of love. Let us immerse ourselves over and over again, a hundred times, a thousand times, in this melody that only the Spirit, only Love, can sing in us.

This prayer is communion and revelation, as much as intercession. In a way, it is Jesus' ascension to his Father. It is not surprising that there are parallels with the Our Father: the tone of intimacy with the Father, glorification of his Name, accomplishment of his Will, deliverance from the Evil One. It is perhaps influenced also by the Jewish liturgy for Yom Kippur.

---

*This is more fully developed in Conference 25 in the liturgical series: 'Return to the Father'.

CHAPTER 17

A. *Glorify your Son (vv. 1–8)*

Aim of the petition	– that your Son may glorify you;
	– that he may give eternal life to all whom you have given him.
Why the petition should be granted	I glorified you on earth
	– by finishing the work;
	– by making your name known;
	– by communicating your words to them.

B. *I pray: that the disciples may be sanctified (vv. 9–19)*

– not for the world (those who are anti-God);

– for those who are yours/mine;

– I am glorified in them.

Now I am coming to you.

Father, protect them in your name . . .

– may they be one as we are one;

– protect them from the Evil One;

– sanctify them in the truth, your Word;

I sanctify myself for them (the meaning of the priestly intercession).

C. *Completion of the mystery of unity and love in all those who are to believe in Jesus (vv. 20–6)*

I ask:

– that they may be one as we are one;

- that you love them as you
  have loved me;
- Father, *I want* them to be
  with me to contemplate your
  glory.

10

The Intercession of the Risen Christ

If anyone does sin,
we have an intercessor [Advocate] with the Father,
Jesus Christ the righteous;
and he is the atoning sacrifice for our sins,
and not for ours only
but also for the sins of the whole world.

(1 John 2:1–2)

The total Christ, the Christ of the whole of the New Testament, is the risen Christ. It is the mediation and the intercession of Christ in glory, the Living One, which really matter. But we must beware of using categories of time, and speaking of before and after. The glorified Christ is no longer in time, he has entered into eternity, which however is not in some sort of after-time.

The prayer of Jesus in glory is no different from the prayer he made in time. It is the same pascal mystery: not just a 'raising of the mind to God', but the passage of the whole of Christ's being to the Father.

The summit of Christ's prayer on earth is the moment in which, in total surrender of himself, body and soul, into the hands of the Father, he leaves this earthly existence and enters into the bosom of the Father. At this moment, the whole of Christ's desire, and his tension towards the Father are answered, in the Father's glorifying embrace.

Raised up above the world on the cross, Jesus thinks only of the work of redemption. He has prayed for his executioners, forgiven the thief, and given his mother to the disciple; and now his spirit leaves even the human beings he came to save, and given to the Father alone. He has only to abandon himself to God for men and women to be saved.

The Church is born in this silence of Christ, at this summit of his prayer, at this moment in which he is completely in the hands of the Father. For us too, now, it is in this silence that we are Christians, and monks. It is our homeland.

This prayer, which is the Son himself, and this answer to prayer, which is the Father, are beyond time, and belong to the extra-temporal moment of eternity, for these temporal modalities are an expression of their divine relationship. At this moment the prayer of the Church, our prayer, is born; it is from there that it springs continually, never separated from its source. In the prayer of the Church, the supreme prayer of Christ at the moment of redemption is spread abroad in time and space: 'Abba, Father, into your hands I commend my spirit.' In his eternal paschal mystery, Jesus is totally turned towards the Father, in a plenitude of self-giving, of answered prayer, and of thanksgiving.

Christ in glory is a temple, and his passover, a prayer; our prayer is made in this temple and in this passover, for we have no other temple, no other passover, than the glorified Christ. We must believe in prayer and in its power of salvation, in the same way that we believe that Christ is the Son of God and that, in his death, he was received into the glory of the Father.

THE LAMB THAT WAS SLAUGHTERED

In the Apocalypse of St John we are given a striking image of Christ in glory, which emphasises the fact that it was in virtue of his sacrifice that he took possession of divine glory.

> Then I saw: between the throne and the four living creatures and among the elders a Lamb standing as if it had been slaughtered . . . He went and took the scroll [of God's plan, of which he is the executor] from the right hand of the One who was seated on the throne . . .
> Then I looked, and I heard the voice of many angels surrounding the throne and the living creatures and the

elders; they numbered myriads of myriads and thousands of thousands, singing with full voice,

> 'Worthy is the Lamb that was slaughtered
> to receive power and wealth and wisdom and might
> and honour and glory and blessing!'

Then I heard every creature in heaven and on earth and under the earth and in the sea, and all that is in them, singing,

> 'To the One seated on the throne and to the lamb
> be blessing and honour and glory and might
> forever and ever!'
>
> (5:6–7, 11–13)

Jesus in glory is now on God's side. His prayer of intercession can only be made in a transcendent way. During his life on earth, with its conditions of time and meritorious free-will, his prayer was situated in that existential distance which lay between his divine will and his human will; and that distance has now been abolished. His human will is completely immersed in the divinity of the Word, in the glory of God. It coincides perfectly with the will of God, which is communicated to Christ in the vision of the Father's plan of love, which Jesus, in his glorified humanity, executes in the regime of time.

Thus we rediscover the real nature of the prayer of intercession, which is the accomplishment of God's will of love, the communication of his being, through the co-operation of the will of his creature. The human will of Christ in glory, united to the Word, embraces God's plan in its entirety, in the whole of its extension throughout time and space.

CHRIST: SOURCE OF LIFE, OF PURE LIGHT AND LOVE, IN PLENITUDE

Having conquered death, Jesus stands before the heavenly throne. It is through the total gift of himself unto death that he has conquered, and he displays the marks of his sacrifice, the emblems of his love. All has now been accomplished. Jesus no longer merits. Now there is only the eternal reality of his love, manifested in his glorified body and in his silent prayer that the salvation he has won should be accomplished in all who believe in him. The Father has already answered his prayer in principle, by raising Jesus from the dead. 'All authority in heaven and on earth has been given to me' (Matthew 28:18). This salvation still has to enter into time, and be received or rejected by each individual liberty. Even the prayer of Jesus in glory cannot force someone to accept his love. In this, his prayer shares in the poverty of almighty Love.

A PRIEST FOREVER

The letter to the Hebrews helps us to understand these things better. Intercession is an expression of the priestly mediation of Christ. But it is through the consecration of his Passion and resurrection that Jesus becomes priest. He is mediator of a New Covenant, and priest forever in his humanity, not as it was on earth, but in its glorified state. In heaven, for all eternity he makes a unique offering to the Father of the sacrifice which is the consummation of his life and the eternal incarnation of his love.

Sent among human beings by the Father, he becomes by his ascension the one who is sent by human beings to God. Having entered into the divine sanctuary, Christ thus 'always lives to make intercession for them' (Hebrews 7:25). He does this not by a succession of requests and fragmented prayers, but by the gift of himself, eternally and totally offered in the silence of his love for the Father.

The intercession of Christ, like his priesthood, is eternal. Fixed in the eternal gift of the Son, it embraces potentially the whole extent of time.

> The Lord has sworn and will not change his mind, 'You are a priest forever' ... Furthermore, the former priests were many in number, because they were prevented by death from continuing in office; but he holds his priesthood permanently, because he continues forever. Consequently

he is able for all time to save those who approach God through him, since he always lives to make intercession for them. (Hebrews 7:21–5)

Freed from the limits of time and space, that he had assumed for love of the world, the Son of God, true human being but truly glorified, intercedes for us in a single eternal act, sure and efficacious.

Jesus is enthroned at God's right hand forever, and through him we can draw near to the Father who has bound himself to us in a New Covenant sealed in the blood of his Son. Jesus, our precursor, has entered into heaven itself, the true sanctuary, 'now to appear in the presence of God on our behalf' (Hebrews 9:24).

THE PRAYER OF THE RISEN CHRIST WITHIN US

We will follow him, if we persevere. We are already there with him, if we really believe.

God who is rich in mercy, out of the great love with which he loved us even when we were dead through our trespasses, made us alive together with Christ . . . and raised us up with him and seated us with him in the heavenly places in Christ Jesus. (Ephesians 2:4–6)

In Christ, our head, we have already entered into the sanctuary of God, but in the half-light of faith. The eternal prayer of Christ is already living in us. There is a prayer of silence and of pure presence which is perhaps an eminent form of the prayer of supplication, and a hidden participation in the prayer of Jesus in heaven. Perhaps this is the 'prayer in secret' mentioned in St Matthew's Gospel. Let us not think to share in it too easily, if our human hearts do not bear the marks of the Passion, and are not as it were transformed by the Spirit of Love, and if our will does not embrace completely the will of God. Nor can we aspire to it too exclusively: first, we have to learn how to ask for things in prayer, in a concrete way, and we need the support of this kind of prayer at all times. We are not in heaven, but are pilgrims on earth. And, in any case, there is always a place for thanksgiving, praise, and adoration. But at all times we have to try to become more open to the presence within us of Christ who is Prayer.

> So if you have been raised with Christ, seek the things that are above, where Christ is, seated at the right hand of God. Set your minds on things that are above, not on things that are on earth, for you have died, and your life is hidden with Christ in God. When Christ who is your life is revealed, then you also will be revealed with him in glory.
>
> (Colossians 3:1–4)

Prayer is the respiration of our being, hidden with Christ in God. It is silence of the mystery that we are; or cry of the hope of things unseen, of a waiting which is not yet fully consummated. At such times, prayer rises from the depth of our heart, revealing to us who we are: a prayer that comes from beyond us, and yet which is within us, a prayer which is the manifestation of a love and a will which are mysteriously at one with God, and supremely efficacious. This is the work of the other Advocate promised by Jesus (John 14:17).

THE INTERCESSION OF THE SPIRIT

> 'If you love me, you will keep my commandments. And I will ask the Father, and he will give you another Advocate, to be with you forever. This is the Spirit of truth . . . ' (John 14:15–17)

Jesus will ask the Father. In the priestly prayer we see the content of this supplication, which will last for all eternity. Now that he has entered into the glory of God, Jesus, by his prayer, is source of the Spirit, who will come and continue the work of redemption, and complete all sanctification. It is only after the passover of the Lord that the Spirit is given in plenitude. So there is a perfection of Christ's intercession, a plenitude of its efficacy, that is attained only in heaven.

Likewise the Spirit helps us in our weakness; for we do

not know how to pray as we ought, but that very Spirit intercedes with sighs too deep for words. And God, who searches the heart, knows what is the mind of the Spirit, because the Spirit intercedes for the saints according to the will of God. (Romans 8:26–7)

The intercession of the Spirit in our heart corresponds to the intercession of Jesus in heaven; both are in complete accord with the will, the love of the Father. Listening attentively to the Spirit within us, and the delicate receptivity to prayer with which he inspires us, puts our prayer at one with the will of the Father. Keeping our eyes fixed on Jesus in heaven gives us the confidence that we are loved and welcomed in Christ by the One to whom we are praying.

If God is for us, who is against us? He who did not withhold his own Son, but gave him up for all of us, will he not with him give us everything else? Who will bring any charge against God's elect? It is God who justifies. Who is to condemn? It is Christ Jesus who died, yes, who was raised, who is at the right hand of God, who indeed intercedes for us! (Romans 8:31–4)

Nothing can separate us from the love of God, manifested in Christ Jesus. The One who is totally Other has become infinitely close. That is the source of our confidence and of our prayer.

11

Paul: From Supplication to Adoration

> There is no longer Jew or Greek, there is no longer slave or free, there is no longer male and female; for all of you are one in Christ Jesus. (Galatians 3:28)

At the basis of Paul's faith is the great intuition of the unity of the Body of Christ which englobes the whole of humanity and transcends all social and human categories. Such is the solidarity of Jesus with those who believe in him, and who believe that what is done to one is done to the other. This is why it is such a pressing duty to work for the good of our brothers and sisters, for their salvation, which is their ultimate good (1 Corinthians 9:1b).

> 'Saul, Saul, why do you persecute me?'
> 'Who are you, Lord?'
> 'I am Jesus, whom you are persecuting.'
> (Acts 9:5)

For love of Christ, Paul will be an apostle.

A second basic intuition is that of salvation through faith in Jesus Christ, and not through the Law.

> For him – Jesus Christ my Lord – I have suffered the loss of all things, and I regard them as rubbish, in order that I may gain Christ and be found in him, not having a righteousness of my own that comes from the law, but one that comes through faith in Christ, the righteousness from God based on faith. (Philippians 3:8–9)

Justice cannot be obtained as wages, nor can it be the fruit of our own efforts: it can only be received from the gratuitous, merciful love of God. So the action of God is of prime importance in apostolic activity.

> What then is Apollos? What is Paul? Servants through whom you came to believe, as the Lord assigned to each. I planted, Apollos watered, but God gave the growth. So neither the one who plants nor the one who waters is anything, but only God who gives the growth. (1 Corinthians 3:5-7)

God is all that matters!

The domain of faith is not the domain of human wisdom, but of the power and wisdom of God; and this is foolishness, weakness, and scandal for human beings (1 Corinthians 1). For our struggle is not against enemies of flesh, but against the spirits of evil. Only spiritual weapons are effective: the strength of God, the shield of faith, the sword of the Spirit, prayer, truth (Ephesians 6:10–20). So, at the heart of Paul's apostolic activities is that which links him directly to God: prayer.

PRAY WITHOUT CEASING

Paul is so ardent that he wants prayer to be continual.

> Pray without ceasing; give thanks in all circumstances. (1 Thessalonians 5:18)

> Do not worry about anything, but in everything by prayer and supplication with thanksgiving let your requests be known to God. (Philippians 4:6)

He himself sets us an example. In the Acts of the Apostles we see him praying in all the important circumstances of his life,* and we see the same thing in his relation to others.

---

*Acts 9:11; 13:3; 14:23; 16:25; 20:36; 21:5; 22:17; 28:8; 28:15.

THANKSGIVING AND SUPPLICATION

You will have noticed that Paul's supplication is nearly always accompanied by thanksgiving. Paul learned how to pray with the psalms. Supported by the remembrance of favours already received, his faith anticipates the answer to his prayer with thanksgiving.

He gives the impression of living in constant wonder at the work of God, starting his prayers and letters with words of thanksgiving, and punctuating them with praise and blessing: 'Blessed be the Lord and Father of our Lord Jesus Christ, the Father of mercies . . . ' (2 Corinthians 1:3; Ephesians 1:3; Philippians 1:3; etc.). This is often followed by a contemplation, in the form of a hymn, of the marvels accomplished by the Father, in Christ. 'He has blessed us in Christ with every spiritual blessing in the heavenly places, just as he chose us in Christ before the foundation of the world . . . ' (Ephesians 1:3–13).

Then follows the prayer of petition: 'I pray that the God of our Lord Jesus Christ, the Father of glory, may give you a spirit of wisdom and revelation as you come to know him, so that the eyes of your heart may be enlightened . . . ' (Ephesians 1:17–18).

Paul's supplication is the fruit of his contemplation, in which he discovers its deepest object: in the midst of innumerable difficulties, the progress of the Word of God in the heart of Christians, and through them, and by them also, its progress in the world.

His prayer does not remain vague. He prays for particular communities, or persons, or for a precise intention, but always, more or less directly, in view of a spiritual benefit.

THE COMBAT OF PRAYER

Prayer is a combat. The apostolic life is one great battle. It is a battle, because it is an activity of giving birth. 'My little children,' Paul says to the Galatians, 'you for whom I am again in the pain of childbirth until Christ is formed in you' (4:19).

We were gentle among you, like a mother tenderly caring for her own children. So deeply do we care for you that we are determined to share with you not only the gospel of God but also our own selves, because you have become very dear to us . . . We dealt with each one of you like a father with his children, urging and encouraging you . . . (1 Thessalonians 2:7–8, 11–12)

It is love that gives life, and prayer is the language of love. Prayer is at the heart of the combat for Christ.

We find in St John's first letter: 'If you see your brother or sister committing what is not a mortal sin, you will ask, and God will give life to such a one' (1 John 5:16).

The apostolic Church repeats Paul's cry to us every day:

Join me in earnest prayer to God. (Romans 15:30)

Epaphras is always wrestling in his prayers on your behalf, so that you may stand mature and fully assured. (Colossians 4:12)

This combat of prayer is not easy. It demands a recentring of our little ego in relation to Christ, and a determination to take upon ourselves the whole weight of the burdens of our brothers: sharing, for example, through an interior experience in the depths of our heart, in their sin, their lack of faith, their inability to love. By our acceptance, may it be transformed into supplication. 'I am now rejoicing in my sufferings for your sake, and in my flesh I am completing what is lacking in Christ's afflictions for the sake of his body, that is, the Church' (Colossians 1:24).

PRAYER AND THE SPIRIT

The exigency of constant prayer, fired by ardent, deep, courageous love, can frighten us. But there is the Holy Spirit.

Continual prayer does not consist in a continuous formulation of explicit prayers. Before all, it is a question of being: the reality of our life hidden with Christ in God (Colossians

3:3). It is the Spirit who has been poured forth into our hearts, and is dwelling there. The Spirit makes us children of God. Through him we cry 'Abba, Father': explicitly sometimes, but more often, and better, implicitly, to the extent that we are living in the presence of God and according to the Spirit, that is, in accordance with our being as children of God in Christ. Sometimes too, 'the Spirit helps us in our weakness, for we do not know how to pray as we ought; but that very Spirit intercedes with sighs too deep for words . . . ' (Romans 8:26), always for the Church, and according to God.

The Spirit who is the bond of love, is the ever-flowing, ever fresh, wellspring of prayer. Prayer is more than human words; it is the movement towards God of the knowledge and love that God alone, finally, awakens in our hearts. It is only through the Spirit that we can confess that Jesus is Lord. 'Pray in the Spirit at all times in every prayer and supplication. To that end keep alert and always persevere in supplication for all the saints. Pray also for me . . . ' (Ephesians 6:18–19).

And let us remember the beautiful image of what our Christian life lived together in the Spirit of Christ could be:

> Let the word of Christ dwell in you richly; teach and admonish one another in all wisdom; and with gratitude in your hearts sing psalms, hymns, and spiritual songs to God. And whatever you do, in word or deed, do everything in the name of the Lord Jesus, giving thanks to God the Father through him. (Colossians 3:16–17)

PRAYER AND ABANDON

But sometimes God does not seem to listen to our prayers, and at first, at least, we do not understand. The ways of God widen our hearts:

> . . . A thorn was given me in the flesh, a messenger of Satan to torment me, to keep me from being too elated. Three times I appealed to the Lord about this, that it

would leave me, but he said to me, 'My grace is sufficient for you, for my power is made perfect in weakness.'

(2 Corinthians 12:7–9)

Then there is this other thorn, in Paul's heart this time. Chapters 9, 10 and 11 of the letter to the Romans give us a moving example of a prayer-contemplation-supplication, grappling with the destiny of the Jewish people, a mystery that caused Paul so much sorrow. 'I could wish that I myself were accursed and cut off from Christ for the sake of my own people, my kindred according to the flesh . . . ' (Romans 9:3). He goes over and over the enigma, trying to understand, but finally abandons himself to trust and faith in the love of God:

O the depth of the riches and wisdom and knowledge of God! How unsearchable are his judgements and how inscrutable are his ways! . . . For from him and through him and to him are all things. To him be glory forever. Amen.

(Romans 11:33, 36)

The last word of supplication is abandon, in adoration.

12

Holy Mary, Mother of God,
Pray for Us, Sinners

When writing this conference, I prayed to Our Lady to help me to do it well: just as I have prayed to her so often, in the big events and the smaller ones, throughout my life. 'Holy Mary . . . ' In our home, every evening after dinner, everyone, including guests and visitors, used to kneel down to say the rosary. There were the comic moments sometimes, and laughter, but that didn't matter. Mary was at home with us, and was one of us.

She is at home in this way in so many Christian families and Christian hearts all over the world, and in every generation. It is comforting for us to be able to turn to a mother, and one so close to our lives and to our hearts, someone so powerful before God! Let us try to think a while on this spontaneous reflex that we have as Christians, which is linked to the firm conviction that Mary's intercession for us to God is efficacious. This is certainly founded on the basic belief in the communion of saints, this solidarity in good and in evil which binds us all together in the same drama of creation, sin and redemption. Each of us is responsible for all, but everyone in his own place, according to the grace he has received from God and the role he is called to play in the salvation of humankind. And here Mary has a very special place, and a role that is the most universal of all, after that of Christ.

There is no doubt that Jesus Christ, the Incarnate Word of God, by his very being as man-God, and through his life of love and the complete gift of himself unto death for us, is the Way, the Truth and the Life. He is the redeemer, and the sole mediator between God and human beings. He joins heaven and earth, and opens the way to the Father in the Spirit, giving us, in him, a share in the eternal life of God. All grace is given in him, and there is nothing that anyone else can add. As for us, we can only draw on this, for ourselves and for our brothers and sisters. For it is God's good pleasure not to save us completely on his own, without our co-operation. His plan is to gather redeemed humanity into one Body in Christ, and it is as members of this Body, and of his people, that he looks on us: as members who are dependent upon one another, and source of the Spirit for one another. It is God alone who gives the Spirit through Jesus, but once given, we communicate the Spirit to one another. In this way, we are mediators for our brothers and sisters.

This does not mean that there are some who are interposed between God and their brothers, preventing them from having immediate access to God and his grace, and to the sole Mediator. There is not a series of authorities that one has to go through before eventually reaching God. Christ became man, in the fullest sense, and the Spirit has been poured into our hearts, that we might have immediate proximity with Christ and immediate access to the Father. Our brothers are with us, and beside us, but because of this gift of the Spirit we are truly united to them in a real reciprocity; we are united together before the living God in the holy communion of the redeemed.

This also applies to Mary. She is on our side, in relation to Christ. She too, as the first of the redeemed, receives everything in anticipation of, and in consideration of, the saving grace of Christ. She is not interposed between ourselves and Christ, as it is sometimes said, as if, being a pure creature, she was more accessible to us, nearer to us, than Jesus. On the contrary, her role in God's plan is to give him to us as our brother, and to eliminate the distance; she is a mother, bringing us to birth in him, bringing him to birth in us.

Having said that, Mary's role is deeper, more vast, and more decisive in the history of salvation, than that of any other human being. What is this role? Her role during her life on earth can help us to understand what she is for us now, in heaven. The meaning of her life here below is precisely that which has now taken on eternal value, on her entry into the finality of her heavenly glory.

It is striking to see how little the personality of Mary is manifested exteriorly. Her face as an individual human being is effaced in the task to which she is called. Before the Incarnation Mary was simply a member of her people. She actualises in her person the abstract personification of Israel, the Daughter of Zion. We see in Mary, in her poverty, her humility, and her total obedience to the Word of God and to his command, the purest expression of the expectation of the messianic promise. The same can be said of her prayer. Mary expects all from God alone, and it is from him that she receives all, for herself, for her people, and for the whole of humanity.

The whole mystery of God is in his Word, the gift of his Word through the Spirit. This event dominates all the rest. Mary becomes the mother of Jesus, the Word: the mother of God. This is not brought about by a unilateral act of God, but involves the co-operation of Mary, of her liberty and her faith. In saying 'yes' to the angel of the Annunciation, Mary accepts the whole plan of the salvation of humanity in Christ. At this point in time, she alone represents us all. There is a universal dimension* to her total consent to the Father's plan of mercy. Mother of Jesus in her flesh, she is also mother of the Church, and of us all who are the Church, in the Spirit.

Then we see her carrying Jesus in her womb to the precursor, John the Baptist, to be recognised by him. She presents the child to the Father in the Temple. She draws Jesus' attention to the lack of wine at the wedding in Cana, and almost against Jesus' will, so to speak, provokes his first miracle by her very human concern. She stays at a distance from Jesus' public life, in a hidden silent presence, returning beside him when his hour comes, when nearly all others have abandoned him. At the foot of the cross she becomes our mother in plenitude, in her sorrowful consent to her son's death for us. 'Here is your

---

*Mary's consent was universal in extension, but, on the level of knowledge, it would seem, it was indistinct: she did not know each one of the redeemed individually.

mother' (John 19:27). It is to her that Jesus entrusts us, when he is dying. When the Spirit is poured out upon the praying community at Pentecost, the effective realisation of Mary's role as mother of the Church begins. Then she is corporally assumed into heaven and seated at the right hand of her son, where she continues her task until the end of time.

It is to this risen Mary, in the glory of God, that we pray. She is queen, but, even more, she is mother. She gives us an insight into the tenderness of God in a way that only a woman can do.

In the light of the beatific vision, in God, Mary knows each one of us individually; for her role in God's plan of salvation concerns all of us individually. The saints in heaven know, in God, the objects of their concern on earth. In her total union with Christ, Mary loves us with the love of Christ. All the treasures of her feminine sensitivity are engaged in her love for us, for, unlike the other saints, her body is already glorified. It is in all her humanness that she responds to us, to our joys, and our hopes, and our sufferings. She knows each one of us, she loves each one of us, and she prays and intercedes for us. This is absolutely certain; but what does it really mean?

It is a misplaced anthropomorphism to oppose the justice of God to the maternal tenderness of Mary. Mary is totally transparent to the light of God. Her maternal love is only a reflection of God's maternal love, which is neither distinct from, nor opposed to his justice. The graces that God gives us through the hands of Mary are not begrudgingly extorted from him. Rather, it is God himself who has freely chosen a certain order through which to bestow his graces on us, by the means and the persons he has created and chosen for this. He wanted to give Mary to us as our mother, and to create the Body of Christ with her co-operation, which is totally subordinate to the action of Christ, but, at its level, absolutely real and universal.

Mary's 'yes' has passed into eternity. She says 'yes' eternally to the whole unique and immense universe of redemption, in which we are all englobed in Jesus Christ. Our salvation depends on this 'yes' now, in the same way as it did at a given point in history.

However, there is this difference, perhaps, between the role of Mary during her life on earth and her role now in heaven. The limitations of Christ as child and Christ as a grown man are now transcended in the glory of the resurrection. So also is the exteriority which inevitably existed here on earth between two beings of flesh and blood, however great was the love between them. Now, in glory, Mary exercises her mediation not so much from beside Christ (as at Cana for example), than in Christ, and through him. Not only are all the resources employed in her mediation a unique and complete gift of the one Mediator, but Mary's whole situation is transformed by her state of total communion and total interiority with regard to Christ. They are completely united in their action regarding us.

We have already looked at the general law concerning intercession. Its source is in God. It is the merciful love of God that reaches out to us through the heart of the one who is praying. The efficacy of prayer is in the measure of its transparency to the action of God. So it is easy to understand the efficacy of the prayer of Mary, whose heart, from the very moment of her conception, was of crystal purity, a pure reflection of the heart of God. What God wants is what Mary wants, and that is absolute. Mary's desires, in her prayer, are the desires of God, and as such, are full of divine power. There is one Source, one Light, one Love. So the prayer of Mary knows the same mysterious limits as the power of God: the limits of his respect for our liberty, and the mystery of his gracious election.

The contemplative life, and especially contemplative prayer, are simply an echo, or better, perhaps, a participation in Mary's 'yes' to the life of the Word engendered in her by the mysterious overshadowing of the Spirit. The monk, who is trying with his whole being to enter into this new life, has perhaps more need than others of the presence of Mary in his solitude. It is easy to understand why the place of Mary has been so important in our Order, from the very beginning. Apart from the stories which uphold this, it is the reflection of an essential requirement of the contemplative life.

There are some who are unhappy about any multiplicity in

our relation to God. They are even uncomfortable with Christ himself sometimes. This attitude belies an ignorance of the role of Christ and of Mary, and also of the Church, which is simply to bring us close to God in a way that is immediate, but sacramental, and adapted to our limited, incarnate means of receiving him. In all simplicity and humility, let us ask for help from the Mother whom Christ has given us.

Holy Mary, Mother of God, pray for us sinners, now and at the hour of our death. Now, in this here and now which is the real place where we can meet God. It is in the here and now that we need God's grace to soften the hardness of our hearts, and make them capable of an unconditional, unreserved 'yes' to the work of the Spirit within us: of an acceptance in faith of all the events and circumstances of the path willed for us by God. Not yesterday or tomorrow, but 'yes' to today, to the concrete here and now.

Holy Mary, pray for us, sinners. There are obstacles in us to this 'yes', deep and tenacious obstacles. We want to abandon our old selves, but there is a whole army noisily warring against us: our excessive self-assertion, our aggressiveness, and our cupidity at all levels, sensual, affective, and intellectual. We stubbornly defend our little autonomy. We hang on to ourselves, resisting anything that calls us beyond our own ideas, our plans, and, in short, our little ego.

Holy Mary, pray for us sinners, now and at the hour of our death: at the hour of our last and greatest opportunity when we can put our whole being into the hands of our 'yes', or into the hands of our 'no'; at that hour when the labour of our coming to birth in Christ will be completed, happily we hope, and we will pass in the Spirit to the Father.

Every moment of our life, each here and now, is pregnant with this final moment, and must be lived in the perspective of this final moment, which will, essentially, be the same.

Mary, you are mother, you are our mother, the one whose task it is to communicate Life: Christ himself.

Be close to us, Mary, to support and protect the growth of Christ within us at each 'now' of our lives, and to strengthen us and help us when the hour has come for our last passage into Life.

13

Sharing on Prayer in the
Name of Jesus

'If in my name you ask me for anything, I will do it.'
(John 14:14)

The reader is invited to reflect on and, perhaps, write down
what it means for her or him to pray in the name of Jesus,
before (or after) reading what each of the novices shares on
this point.

Peter
There are several levels in the prayer of Jesus.

1. The prayer of Jesus to his Father when he was on earth.
   We make this prayer ours as we say, 'Our Father', because,
   by grace, we are truly his sons.
2. Prayer that is addressed to Jesus, our Lord and our God.
   As Peter says in Acts 4:12: 'There is salvation in no one
   else, for there is no other name under heaven given among
   mortals by which we must be saved.'
3. The 'Jesus Prayer': a short prayer containing the name of
   Jesus ('Jesus', 'Lord Jesus', or 'Lord Jesus Christ, Son
   of God, have mercy on me a sinner') constantly repeated
   in one's heart. It is a simple method of prayer that has been
   widespread in the East especially, but also, today, in the
   West.

For me personally, it is the gentle resonance of the name of
'Jesus' that strikes a chord, and the cosmic dimension of the
invocation of his name: it is the prayer of Jesus in us, the prayer
of the whole Christ, which includes the whole of humanity and

the cosmos (Ephesians 1:22). I have, in particular, a strong feeling of communing in the prayer of the Church, on earth and in heaven, the plenitude of Christ.

James

Sinful human beings try to approach God. Jesus pays our debt, and takes us to the Father. He is the door through which we enter. To pray in the name of Jesus is to recall this redemption, and come to the Father under the wings of his Son, who makes us worthy of God. Of myself, I am nothing; Jesus is my only access to the Father and to his love.

John

'If in my name you ask me for anything, I will do it.' Jesus wants us to ask him for all we need, which, in the end, is the Holy Spirit. But he wants us to do his will, too . . . Jesus is the way: that is, prayer and observance of God's commandments.

- When I am united to Jesus through faith and love, every prayer I make is in the name of Jesus: the Father sees Jesus in me.
- Just calling on his name materially, like the Jewish exorcists, is not enough. The Father sees his Son in the one who does his will. Otherwise it is a prayer devoid of power.
- To begin with, Anthony, one of the first Christian hermits, was the friend of God. At the end of his life, he was transfigured, he had, as it were, become Jesus. And 'he who sees me sees the Father.'
- Jesus, have mercy on me. Come, Lord Jesus, so that, united to you, I can pray for others. Lord, have mercy on us.

Matthew

'If in my name you ask me for anything, I will do it.' I am very struck by these words, here and now. It's about praying in the power of the death, resurrection, and love/faithfulness of Jesus. These are real, lasting facts.

'In my name'. Maybe there are metaphysical implications in

that, but that is not what strikes me at the moment. It is just
the plain statement of these words that impresses me. It's as
though I am casting myself in all confidence into this name.
The promise is efficacious, here and now.

Arsenius

Jesus, that is the call of my vocation, and my response. He is
the Alpha and the Omega. But there's always the risk of my
falling away from him.

- Prayer in the name of Jesus means living his passion in
  everyday life.
- It's Mary's annunciation, her 'yes' said in faith, the visit to
  Elizabeth.
- It is God who loved us, first. God is Love.
- Praying in the name of Jesus means being rooted up from
  oneself, it's loving Jesus, living with him.
- With Saint Theresa of Lisieux, it's putting my sins in the
  heart of Jesus.
- The spiritual life is a laborious ascension, a combat.
- It's living the passion of Jesus, becoming a better person.
- The name of Jesus helps us.
- Our faults don't matter.
- The important thing is to love.

Philip

I just don't know who I pray to or how I pray. I simply hope
there's someone listening to me.

- It's about hoping, persevering.
- The visual, devotional image of a beautiful Jesus no longer
  helps me. It's too small.
- Where, who, what . . . ? I really don't know.
- What matters most in prayer is purity of heart, whence
  union and presence.
- Prayer (as I understand or want it) can be the main obstacle
  to real prayer.
- For me, it's very simple words: Father, Mother . . .

Gabriel

I don't feel that I pray in the name of 'Jesus'. I haven't the faith to do that.

One day in my parish church, we were listening to the Gospel of the healing of the paralytic: 'Stand up and walk'. There was an invalid there just in front of me. I felt moved to order him to do the same thing. But, through lack of faith or human respect, I didn't do it.

- When I pray, I try to see what I want in the light of what Jesus our Saviour wants. If there is conformity, then my prayer is Christian prayer.
- I would like to pray as Jesus prays; and so say 'Father', not 'Jesus'.
- It is only during the celebration of the Eucharist that I feel that my lack of faith is surmounted. Jesus is there, present; my prayer intentions are offered in him, efficaciously.
- I find it difficult to live in a felt, incarnate faith, faith in the victory of Easter. That will come, one day; for the time being it's a naked faith.

Benedict

'Jesus', that's a name that's meant to be sung, like Jerusalem in the Gregorian antiphons; there are harmonics between *Yerou-shalaïm* and *Yeshoua*, Jesus.

In Zen calligraphy, the written word is everything: with no interiority 'behind' it. The name itself is self-sufficient, in its place, with no inside or outside. The whole truth can only be expressed completely in a name. (I must admit that I don't know it, and that, if I did, I would not be able to say it.) Gregorian chant is the oral calligraphy of the West.

Jesus: that's something that has to become incarnate . . . Like when, out of love, you write down the name of someone you love, just to see it . . . so it's a beloved name; it's something to be eaten; to masticate. We can pray the name of Jesus. I remember an old lady in the church of Our Lady of Victories. She repeated, over and over again, 'Jesus, O gentle Jesus, O my Jesus . . .' That made such an impression on the young intellectual that I was. In prayer it's enough just to repeat the name of Jesus. 'Jesus', the Saviour. 'Christ', the Anointed One. A living Person who saves; knowing his name means we can call upon him. It's fantastic.

Faith, it's adherence to a Person, more than to a doctrine. The Church is not the same thing as a doctrine. She is Church through her bond with a living Person in the Eucharist.

In the whole of the Old Testament people have tried to get God to pronounce his name (for example, in the combat of Jacob with the angel). God gave them a name that distinguished him from other 'gods', but it left him veiled in mystery: the tetragram YHWH. This is expressed in the Kabbala which says that if, one day, someone really does pronounce the unpronounceable,* infinite name of *Elohim*, the earth will fall to pieces.

Note: At first the Israelites pronounced the tetragram; then, through respect, did so less and less, up till the second exile. Afterwards it was no longer pronounced at all (it was replaced by *Adonaï*, or *Elohim*, because the vowels were not written in Hebrew, and the correct pronunciation had been lost).

14

Prayer in the Name of Jesus

In order to deepen our understanding of prayer in the name of Jesus, we must first study the notion of name in the Bible.

THE OLD TESTAMENT*: YAHWEH

Far from being simply a conventional designation, the name expresses the particular role of a being in the universe. Adam exercises his domination over the animals by giving each of them a name (Genesis 2:20).

In every people, the name given to the divinity is very important. The Babylonians give fifty names to their supreme god, Mardouk, to consecrate his victory at the time of creation. The Canaanites have the generic term of Baal, meaning 'master' (of one or other particular place), which covers all their different gods.

For the Israelites, the God of the patriarchs is called 'Shaddaï' (the God of the mountain), 'the Terror of Isaac', 'the Strong One of Jacob', etc., or he refuses to give his name, as with Jacob (Genesis 32:29). The reality expressed in the name is the relationship of God to a person or a place; God in himself cannot be named.

Then one day, at Horeb, God reveals his name to Moses: 'I am who I am' (Exodus 3:13–16; 6:3). This is the tetragram, Yahweh. It is a name that consecrates the mystery of God, whilst signifying his presence in the midst of the people he has chosen. It is a name which, rightly or wrongly, will be at the centre of a whole line of metaphysical reflection on the concept

---

*See the article on 'The Name', in the *Vocabulaire de Théologie Biblique* by Xavier-Leon Dufour which these notes on the Old Testament summarise.

of being: God, the *ipsum esse subsistens*, the Being who subsists in himself.

For the Israelites, whose concern is religious, Yahweh is the name of the one, true God, whom they adore and serve. Invoking his name is equivalent to worshipping and praying God. His name is sacred, and must not be pronounced in vain (Exodus 20:7), or used for one's own interests. No other god, no other name must be invoked, for his 'name is Jealous' (Exodus 34:14).

God is so identified with his own name, that when he pronounces it, he is speaking of himself. It is this awesome eternal Name that is loved and praised and sanctified (the Psalms contain many examples).

His actions in favour of Israel are 'for his great Name' (Joshua 7:9), 'for the sake of his name' (Ezekiel 20:9), that is, for his glory, that he may be acknowledged as great and holy.

To emphasise the inaccessible and mysterious transcendence of God, 'the Name' suffices to designate him. So it is that the Temple is the place which God has 'chosen as his habitation to put his Name there' (Deuteronomy 12:5), and it is there that the people come into his presence (Exodus 34:23); it is his Name that will sift the nations with the sieve of judgement (Isaiah 30:28). In rabbinic vocabulary, 'the Name', without further precision, designates God.

With ever increasing respect, gradually Judaism does not even dare to pronounce the name revealed at Horeb. When reading aloud, 'Yahweh' is replaced by *Elohim* – God; or more often by *Adonaï* – my Lord. This explains why, in the Greek translation of the Bible, 'Yahweh' is translated as *Kyrios*, Lord, the name which is subsequently consecrated in the New Testament. How curious it is, and sad, that, except for some esoteric groups, Christians in general have lost the sense of the sacredness of the name of Yahweh. The splendour of the name of the Father of Our Lord Jesus Christ has eventually absorbed the first revelation.

THE NEW TESTAMENT*

The name of Jesus

The etymology of the word Jesus means: Yahweh saves. The word indicates Jesus' messianic missions. He manifests the salvation that he brings by actions that testify to his power: expelling demons, healing the sick, raising the dead to life, and giving orders to nature itself. These acts are signs of the coming of the Kingdom of God, of the forgiveness of the Father and of the gift of the Spirit. The supreme action is the death-resurrection of Jesus.

The supernatural power of the name of Jesus

It is the very power that Jesus exercised in his own right that his disciples exercise in his name. We read in the Acts of the explosion of the power of the Spirit in the apostolic Church. It is not a question of another new doctrine, but of the divine power of the reign of God irrupting into our world. The believers are animated by the Spirit, who guides them, and fills them with strength and courage. As Jesus did, and in his name, they expel demons (Acts 19:13; Luke 10:17; Mark 9:38) and heal the sick (Acts 3:6: 'In the name of Jesus Christ of Nazareth, stand up and walk'). Peter and John are interrogated before the Sanhedrin for having healed a lame man in the Temple: 'By what power or by what name did you do this?' Then Peter, filled with the Holy Spirit, said to them, 'This man is standing before you in good health by the name of Jesus Christ of Nazareth, whom you crucified, whom God raised from the dead . . . there is no other name under heaven given among mortals by which we must be saved' (Acts 4:7, 9–10, 12).

Threatened by the Jews, they pray to the Lord: ' "Lord, look at their threats, and grant to your servants to speak your word with all boldness, while you stretch out your hand to heal, and signs and wonders are performed through the name of your holy servant Jesus." . . . and they were all filled with the Holy Spirit and spoke the word of God with boldness' (vv. 29–31).

*The article 'The Name of Jesus in the New Testament' by Père J. Dupont in the *Supplément du Dictionnaire Biblique* contains a detailed study.

But the name of Jesus is not just a magical word that only has to be materially pronounced in order to obtain the desired effect. This is made clear in the misadventure of the itinerant Jewish exorcists. Imitating Paul, they pronounce the name of the Lord Jesus over those possessed by evil spirits, and these spirits then attack them. To bring salvation, the name of Jesus has to be invoked with faith in his person and in his salvific mission. Then, when his name is called upon, it is Jesus himself who becomes present and who acts. It is Jesus himself who is working miracles through the intermediary of his disciples: 'Aeneas, Jesus Christ heals you; get up and make your bed!' (Acts 9:34)

To be precise, it is the risen Christ that we invoke, and who becomes present, the Lord in the state of glory which is now his. When we invoke his name, we confess that Jesus is Lord, that God has raised him from the dead (Romans 10:6–13). Stephen saw 'the glory of God and Jesus standing at the right hand of God' (Acts 7:56). The Christian is 'baptised in the name of the Lord Jesus' (Acts 19:5; 8:16; Romans 6:3) which means that he is Lord. This name expresses the status and mission of the Messiah. The disciples preach the name of Jesus Christ, the Lord, both to the Jews and to the pagans (Luke 24:46–7; Romans 1:4–5). They suffer for the sake of the Name (Acts 5:41). The whole of their lives takes the form of, is transformed by, their faith in this name.

> Whatever you do, in word or deed, do everything in the name of the Lord Jesus, giving thanks to God the Father through him.
> (Colossians 3:17; see also 2 Thessalonians 1:12)

Through centuries, the saints have called upon the name of Jesus in all their needs, especially in their spiritual combat against temptation and the attacks of Satan. They have done so too, speaking more generally, by the constant invocation of his name, to keep the presence of Jesus in their hearts.

When Jesus enters into the glory of the Father, he does not abandon us. 'Remember, I am with you always, to the end of the age' (Matthew 28:20).

He is there where there is faith in his name – among ourselves, for example! 'Where two or three are gathered in my name, I am there among them' (Matthew 18:20).

He offers himself to our love in little ones, in the poor, in our brothers and sisters.

> Whoever welcomes one such child in my name welcomes me. (Matthew 18:5)

> Just as you did it to one of the least of these my brothers [the poor, the strangers, the sick, the prisoners, etc.], you did it to me. (Matthew 25:40)

15

The Name That Is Above Every Other Name

In order to express the new status of Christ brought about by the event of the resurrection, Christian theological reflection has drawn on the Jewish theology of the Name. In attributing the title of Lord to the risen Christ, the authors of the New Testament have been inspired by the Old Testament texts. According to this theology, God has a name of his own which is ineffable, and inseparable from the mystery of his very being. This mystery is symbolised by the empty Holy of Holies in the Temple; any representation would be an idol. This Name is linked to the title of 'Lord', which is the traditional translation of the sacred tetragram (Yahweh), and shares in some way in its mystery.

So we have:

1. The ineffable Name of God, corresponding to his very being which transcends, absolutely, every creature, and any name drawn from our knowledge of creatures, and anything relating to creatures.
2. The sacred Tetragram, Yahweh, the specific name revealed by God himself: it designates God, but does not unveil his mystery: 'I am who I am'.
3. *Kyrios*, Lord, the traditional Greek translation of the tetragram.
4. The name of Lord attributed to the risen Christ, in a way which beforehand was reserved to God alone. So this name is an evocation of the divine mystery which it cannot express, it opens onto silence.

Let us look at some texts of St Paul, and of the author of

the letter to the Hebrews, and of St John, that illustrate this movement.

St Paul celebrates the glorification of Jesus Christ who voluntarily humbled himself to death on a cross.

> Therefore God also highly exalted him and gave him the Name that is above every name, so that at the name of Jesus every knee should bend, in heaven and on earth and under the earth, and every tongue should confess that Jesus Christ is Lord, to the glory of God the Father. (Philippians 2:9–11)

We have to read this text in relation to Ephesians 1:20–1:

> God put this power to work in Christ when he raised him from the dead and seated him at his right hand in the heavenly places, far above all rule and authority and power and dominion, and above every name that is named, not only in this age but also in the age to come.

The exaltation of Jesus above all creation, and above every created name, is expressed in the 'Name above every other name'* conferred upon him by God when he raised him from the dead. This supreme Name cannot be the one that Jesus had since his birth. Its concrete translation is expressed in the title of 'Lord' attributed to him by all creatures: to the Name received by the risen Christ corresponds the confession: 'Jesus Christ is Lord.'

---

*'This name is that of Lord (v. 11); or, more profoundly, it is the ineffable Divine Name which, in the triumph of the risen Christ, is expressed by the title of Lord' (noted by Père Benoît in the *Bible de Jérusalem*).

L. Cerfaux insists on the distinction that has to be maintained between 'the Name that is above every other name', and the title of *Kyrios* 'Lord', that is a consequence of the Name: 'The Name that is above every other name is the root of the sovereignty; it cannot be Kyrios, which in fact expresses this sovereignty; we have to look far beyond this title of Kyrios to a deeper reality, to an inaccessible, ineffable "Name"' (*Le Christ dans la théologie de Paul*, p. 358).

In reality, the same thing can be said of the name 'Yahweh', which designates the ineffable being of God, without actually revealing it.

The Name that Jesus receives is not a simple title: it stands
for the dignity and the mode of being of God himself, that the
title of 'Lord' supposes. 'To me [Yahweh] every knee shall bow,
every tongue shall swear' (Isaiah 45:23). By acknowledging that
the sovereignty of Jesus is specifically divine, he is, at the same
time, being attributed a divine state, a mode of being that
belongs to God alone.

When he became a human being, the Word did not cease to
be God. 'But he emptied himself, taking the form of a slave'
(Philippians 2:7). It is by the resurrection that the humanity of
Jesus attains to its full glory of divine light and divine status.*
'So that at the name of Jesus every knee should bend'. It is not
upon the hypostasis of the Word that these divine honours are
bestowed, but indeed, upon Jesus of Nazareth, the Word in his
risen humanity. It is to Jesus, and to his name, that is, to
the concrete, incarnate person designated by this name, that the
homage of the whole of creation is addressed.

The letter to the Hebrews also speaks of a name received by
Jesus at the time of his resurrection:

> He is the reflection of God's glory and the exact imprint
> of God's very being, and he sustains all things by his
> powerful word. When he had made purification for sins,
> he sat down at the right hand of the Majesty on high,
> having become as much superior to angels as the name he
> has inherited is more excellent than theirs. For to which

---

*'Paschal Christology, which is that of the New Testament in general,
does not reflect from the point of view of the natures of Christ. Con-
sidering things from a more concrete angle, it emphasizes the fact that,
when he rose from the dead, Jesus, in his humanity, took possession of
prerogatives and conditions of existence that are specifically divine. It is
in this sense that he is attributed the "Name" which expresses a mode of
being which is that of God himself. This doctrine is not a direct affirmation of the divinity of the risen Christ, but it clearly supposes it. To
see this as consequential, we have to refer to concepts that the first
Christians did not as yet have' (*Supplément du Dictionnaire Biblique*, col.
534).

of the angels did God ever say, 'You are my Son; today I
have begotten you'? (Hebrews 1:3–5)

Following an exegesis familiar to the first Christians (Acts
13:33; Hebrews 5:5), this verse of the psalm was seen as a
prophecy of the resurrection; it is when Jesus is raised from the
dead that God says to him, 'You are my son; today I have
begotten you' (Psalm 2:7). The sense in which Jesus merits the
name of Son of God in this declaration is so exalted as to
transcend the name of every other creature.

The Apocalypse presents Jesus Christ in the form of a rider
mounted on a white horse:

> Then I saw heaven opened, and there was a white horse! Its
> rider is called Faithful and True, and in righteousness he
> judges and makes war. His eyes are like a flame of fire,
> and on his head are many diadems; and he has a name
> inscribed that no one knows but himself. (Revelation
> 19:11–12)

The appellations of 'Faithful' and 'True' that are given him are
not his real name, which is known to himself alone. This ineffable Name is part of the mystery of God's being. However
there are concrete ways of expressing this ineffable Name; these
are titles given to Christ in glory which express not what he is
in himself, but his relationship to God (the Word), or to the
universe (King). The text continues:

> His name is called the Word of God . . . On his robe and
> on his thigh he has a name inscribed, 'King of kings
> and Lord of lords'. (19:13, 16)

Jesus will communicate this ineffable Name and the reality it
signifies, to those who believe in him.

> 'To everyone who conquers I will give some of the hidden
> manna, and I will give a white stone, and on the white
> stone is written a new name that no one knows except the
> one who receives it.' (2:17–18)

Doubtless this refers to the 'Name that is above every name' that Christ received after his resurrection (Philippians 2:9). The believer will receive communication of the name of his Lord: that is to say, he is called to share in the same dignity and destiny as his Lord.

> 'If you conquer, I will make you a pillar in the temple of my God; you will never go out of it. I will write on you the name of my God, and the name of the city of my God, the new Jerusalem that comes down from my God out of heaven, and my own new name.' (3:12; see also 14:1 and 22:3–4)

SUMMARY

- By raising Jesus from the dead, God makes him Lord (Acts 2:36).
- He gives him part in his divine lordship over all creatures (Philippians 2:10–11).
- He engenders him, declares that he is his own Son (Hebrews 1:5).
- He bestows on him the Name that is above every name (Philippians 2:9; Hebrews 1:4).
- The glorious titles of Jesus are only an expression of this (Revelation 19:12–16).
- Jesus shares his divine dignity with all who believe in him (Revelation 2:17).

These statements give us some glimpse of the depth of the mystery evoked in the name of Jesus Christ, the Lord.

16

When I Say 'Jesus Christ'

When I call upon the name of Jesus Christ, in prayer, this is the faith that I profess:

God incarnate in the human nature of Jesus of Nazareth, in whom the ultimate subject is the divine person of the Word of God.

Jesus Christ, the immediate presence of the invisible God in our world of space and time.

The Son, the radiant image of the Father, eternally engendered by the Father, and source, with him, of the Spirit. He is the manifestation of the Father with a human face, in human history.

A Face that is fully human: the Son accepted the total reality of our human condition – except for sin – with all its finitude, its limits, its succession in time, its subjection to suffering and death. This was the first sacrifice of Love.

A Face of poverty and, on the human level, of impotence in presence of the forces of destruction and evil, respecting their autonomy and their liberty of action.

A Face of absolute faith and trust in the Father and in his will for the eternal happiness of all humanity.

A Face of love and forgiveness freely bestowed, to the point of sacrificing his life for us in total gift.

The promise of eternal life through a sharing of grace in the life of the Father, the Son, and the Holy Spirit.

Promise realised first of all in Jesus, by his resurrection from the dead on Easter morning.

Promise realised, in faith, in each of those who believe, by the gift of his Spirit; pledge already here on earth of the divine life of knowledge and love; power within us for living and for acting in the image of Christ; the bond uniting humankind to form the Church, the Body of Christ, whose sacramental actions are the actions of Christ in the Spirit.

Promise fulfilled in our souls when they come face to face with God in the plenitude of light, at the moment of death, (or after a purification); and fulfilled for the totality of our humanity at the end of time, at the Parousia, the second coming of Christ, when God will be all in all.

When I say Jesus Christ, I proclaim all this.

I profess my faith in God alone. I admit that I am a sinner, radically incapable of loving completely, and of being in truth the creature that I am. Infinitesimal potential of existence, hovering over the void of my contingency, faint light of the spirit barely emerging from matter. There are awakenings of personal liberty, yet imprisoned in so many ways, blind egotism referring everything to myself, ambition to be my own saviour, relying on myself alone; greed, demanding my share of self-assertion and pleasure, as a right, little caring for everyone else, sometimes to their detriment; a wolf for my brother, or a blank wall, afraid of the other, enclosed in the anguish of a sterile solitude . . . a sinner. And yet, still, boundless capacity for love and knowledge! Who will deliver me from my isolation? God alone.

In Jesus Christ, God comes looking for me in my very isolation, he draws near, and hides himself in my very wounds. He dies of them, and it is by means of this death that he breaks the shell of my self-sufficiency, my pride, and my fear. He says: love means dying to yourself, giving yourself to the Other. He does not eliminate suffering and death, neither for himself nor for us. He turns them into the gateway of Life, through which he shows us, and is for us, the Way and the Truth: a life so marvellous and vast that, to enter into it, we have to come out of ourselves totally, and be born again, to pass through the primordial waters over which hovers the Spirit of God.

When I say Jesus Christ, I confess that I myself can do nothing of all this. I can only receive, and give my consent of faith, in total poverty; letting go of the illusion of my own autonomy, so as to be born into the liberty of the Spirit of Christ; and leaving space within myself for the surge of a life, and a love, and a light which are my true self, and yet which are never mine to possess, because they are a gift. Life of God within me, eternal life, which will not pass away.

When I say Jesus Christ, I believe in God alone, I expect everything from him alone. I abandon myself to him, totally. For my life, for the acts and trials of the purification he will give me to endure, as long as it is done in love. For my death, that I envisage calmly and lucidly, seeing in it the Door which is Christ: he who bears my own mortal face, and who is hope of immortality.

I abandon time to him. I entrust the past into the merciful hands of the Father. The future, and my hope itself, insomuch as they are 'elsewhere', I put out of my mind, in order to be with Christ on earth, in order to focus my whole attention on the here and now of my life, opening my hands like a beggar to receive each moment, preciously, as a grace and a creation.

When I say Jesus Christ, I proclaim all this.

I tell of my isolation which has been changed into solitude. Face to face, within me, you are there. It is solitude, for you are hidden; but not isolation. I plunge into the vertiginous spaces of my heart to find myself alone. Completely alone? Where is the Other? One by one I break the images and idols of my mind. The place is empty. Each idol was nothing but a mask of my own face, the face of my selfish desire or of my fear. What is left? My heart of flesh, the trees, the sky, water, fire. Of You, no trace. And yet yes, Christ is there. Presence in the absence. In the void, all things. Humility of God. Immensity of the gift, totally given. Evidence of the invisible . . . visible evidence.

When I say Jesus Christ, to be faithful to him – am I better than him? – I fully assume the task of my human life, with the limits of my mortal humanity. I renounce all evasions of the imagination into somewhere else, something different. I am to live in the real where Jesus lived, and to love there where I am, with the means available, just as they really are.

But when I say Jesus Christ, I tell also of the unfathomable solitude of God, to nothing else comparable, to nothing else measurable. Solitude of the Unique. Solitude that founds all communion. Absolute transcendence. Source and stay of all that exists. He who dwells in inaccessible light, whose Name is above all other names. Silence of infinite plenitude. Very Being, in Itself and by Itself. Father, Son, Spirit. Silence which calls for my silence. Silence of adoration.

When I say Jesus Christ, I tell of the paradox of divine omnipotence revealed in the figure of a man, alone, abandoned, in agony on the cross, who still goes on believing. The Father does not ask us to have faith only in his infinite riches, but also in his stark poverty. The greatest light is revealed in the greatest darkness, in blackest night. On the cross all our idols die, all the gods in our own likeness that we make, and hold on to. We have to lose 'God' in order to find the Father. On the cross we die to our little self, in order to awaken to Love. For Love calls us to love, breathing the Spirit of Love into us, inviting us to the vulnerability of our true selves, to this exit from ourselves towards others, in the image of the Son's going forth in poverty from the Father; and to the gift of welcome we are to offer to our brothers, and even in their sin.

When I say Jesus Christ, I accept that it is not I who live, but Christ who lives in me. The walls of my ego collapse, and, with them, the defences and limits set up by my refusals. I become open to my brothers, and to the whole Body of Christ. I have no right to appropriate my own little this or that, nor to exclude my brother's part. All that is Christ's is mine, and all that is mine belongs to Christ, to the total Christ, and so to my brothers. We have to become what we are, one in Christ, by the same bond of Love that unites the Father and the Son eternally, the Holy Spirit. Just as the solitude of the One God bears fruit in the Word and in Love, so can it be, so must it be, too, of our solitude.

When I say Jesus Christ, I say that this is possible, because Christ is risen from the dead. Seated at the right hand of the Father, he is the source of a new life that he communicates to us through his incarnate acts – that is to say, the sacraments of the Church – and through his Spirit. The Father has given him the Name above every other name, and he, in turn, communicates it to us, written on the white stone that each of us receives in secret.

When I say Jesus Christ, I believe that he comes to us each day to commune with us and uphold us during our earthly journey. I believe that he will come on the last day to establish his Kingdom permanently.

When I say Jesus Christ, I profess my faith that he is the light that enlightens everyone (John 1:9). That he is secretly present in every person of good will: as the Word that stirs every mind that turns to God, and the Spirit that moves every heart that seeks God, that seeks the Absolute, whatever word we use to express it. I believe that the Kingdom of God will embrace all people of all times in the history of humankind. Christ assumed the whole of humanity, which is totally redeemed in him. No one is excluded. His grace, the life of the resurrection, the Spirit, are all present and active in everyone everywhere, beyond any distinctions of place and time.

When I say Jesus Christ, I confess my faith in humanity. In his name, I embrace all that is noble, and good, and profound in the human and spiritual quest of all people, of whatever creed or religion. 'Then people will come from east and west, from north and south, and will eat in the kingdom of God' (Luke 13:29).

When I say Jesus Christ, I proclaim a tremendous optimism; in spite of the disasters and wars, and humankind's obstinate sins, the Kingdom of God will triumph, and will be established over the whole of creation. All will be well, very well, on that day. Nature itself, so too our bodies, will blossom anew, mysteriously transformed by the light of the resurrection, to become redeemed humanity's song of praise to the glory of God. Our prayer, the openness of our hearts to the One who is coming, hastens the coming of his reign, as does also every act accomplished in the charity of the Spirit. For in the Spirit the Kingdom is already given, and is only waiting for us to bring it to realisation.

When I pronounce the name of Jesus Christ, this name contains all this, not discursively, but in an intensity of concentration and immediacy. And if the Spirit leads me imperceptibly into the silence of this Name above every other name, so as to become adoration, in wordless presence of the heart, then this silence says all this, and even more.

Maranatha. Come, Lord Jesus!

Part 2

17

The Life of Prayer

Having been led by the grace of the Spirit into the depths of his own soul, the monk is now ready, not only to serve God, but even to cleave to Him in love.*

I love the second Sunday in Lent so much. It is the Sunday of spiritual transfiguration, seen in the obscure light of the cloud over the mountain. That is our aim: that the whole of our being should be transfigured in the light of God. And this is the way to attain it: to go up onto the mountain alone and enter into the cloud in which God's glory dwells, under the appearance of a devouring fire. It is the cloud of the mystery of God, and the fire of his jealous love which devours everything which separates us from him.

THE GLOBAL VIEW OF THE FATHERS

We are going to focus our attention on the distinctive features of the different stages of the life of prayer; but we must not forget that they are in fact interconnected, and interdependent. Also, we must not isolate times of prayer from the general context of our life. These are very modern errors, and very damaging ones too.

We are contemplatives, and first of all by living a life in which everything, down to the most material aspects of it, is organised in a way which will facilitate and express our turning to God in faith and love. All our activities are modulations of a unique theme. This is especially true of our interior activities. Reading, meditation, prayer and contemplation are all intimately linked

---

*S.R. 3, 2.

together. For the Fathers, these were the different moments of every period of *lectio divina*. They regarded contemplation as an act which could happen during reading, at office, or at a time of manual work: an act which was generally of limited duration, but which was always ready to surface.

There is a tendency in modern thought to regard contemplation as a state of mental prayer, some superior and extraordinary degree of it, to be cultivated by very specialized means, instead of seeing it as the normal fruit of a life filled with God. For very busy people living in the world, it is justifiable to a certain extent to make a specialization of contemplation and its technical aspects. But we would do better to embrace the vital simplicity of the ancient monks. In practice, this means always remaining open and available to the impulsion of the Spirit, who can bring us to a halt, anywhere, and at any time, and make us know that God is God (Psalm 45:11).

Even if we have not the grace to be in a state of habitual contemplation, we will surely receive from time to time the grace of acts of contemplation, if we are present enough to God, and open to the murmur of the Spirit.

In the *Ladder for Monks*, written about 1145, Guigo II, one of the first Priors of the Chartreuse, has given us a programme which is still acceptable for our own times.

> Reading is the careful study of the scriptures, concentrating all one's powers on it. Meditation is the busy application of the mind to seek with the help of one's own reason for knowledge of hidden truth. Prayer is the heart's devoted turning to God to do away evil and obtain what is good. Contemplation is when the mind is in some sort lifted up to God, and held above itself, so that it tastes the joys of everlasting sweetness.
>
> Reading seeks for the sweetness of a blessed life, meditation perceives it, prayer asks for it, contemplation tastes it . . . Reading as it were puts food whole into the mouth, meditation chews it and breaks it up, prayer extracts its flavour, contemplation is the sweetness itself which gladdens and refreshes. (Ch. 2)

Reading, meditation, prayer and contemplation are so linked together, each one working also for the others, that the first degrees are of little or no use without the last, whilst the last can never or hardly ever be won without the first. For what is the use of spending one's time in continuous reading, turning the pages of the lives and sayings of holy men, unless we can extract nourishment from them by chewing and digesting this food so that its strength can pass into our inmost heart? . . . Again, what use is it to anyone if he sees in his meditation what is to be done, unless the help of prayer and the grace of God enable him to achieve it? . . . From this we learn that if meditation is to be fruitful, it must be followed by devoted prayer, and the sweetness of contemplation may be called the effect of prayer . . . To obtain contemplation without prayer would be rare, even miraculous.

CONTEMPLATION

As the words 'mystical' and 'contemplation' are often used in rather a vague way, let us be clear from the start about their meaning. This will give us a clear idea of our aim.

The knowledge of God given in infused contemplation is completely different to that which can be attained through the ordinary exercise of our faculties, even when enlightened by faith. It is a knowledge of love, the fruit of love and of a special impulsion of the Holy Spirit, a simple, global, intuitive view of God and of the things of God. It is not an act that we can produce at will, as is the case in the act of faith or ordinary prayer, in which grace leaves us our initiative and our usual mode of operation.

The mystical life is a life in which the action of the gifts of the Spirit are predominant. This life, in its fulness, is one in which all the gifts are exercised, but there are different vocations. Sometimes the gifts of the active life are more in evidence (counsel, force, etc.), at other times we see the gifts of contemplation (intelligence and wisdom). But we usually find infused contemplation present in the saints, in one form or another (and there are some very hidden forms of it).

We who are called to a way of life directed towards contemplation, are by the very fact called to infused contemplation, at least in some remote way. This does not mean that every Carthusian will automatically receive this grace. You can be holy without ever leaving the paths of ordinary prayer. But it seems to me that, insofar as it depends on us, we ought at least to have a maximum of openness to the action of the Spirit, and to the light which, in the plan of his providence, he wishes to communicate to us. The important thing is to go forward in truth and in the love of God. The Lord will give us a knowledge of himself which will help us to love him as much as possible, if we are faithful to doing as best we can with the help of his grace.

18

The First Passage

Let us look at our general plan. The Places of passage are what most interest us. There is the first passage from a worldly life to a fervent religious life, a second passage and the third passage to living the theological virtues in a purer way.

If the life of Christ, the paschal mystery, is to come to its plenitude in us, we have to be careful not to get stuck in these places of passage. Many come through the first, less through the second, and few through the third.

We are going to study them especially from the point of view of prayer, but without losing sight of life as a whole. Prayer is the raising of the soul to God, to adore him, praise him, etc., or to ask him for something, or indeed simply to love him and converse with the One by whom we know ourselves to be loved. Prayer is always an activity of faith, preceded, given form, and upheld by the grace of God, which alone makes it possible. It is by the Spirit that we cry 'Father' (Romans 8:15). Prayer is the fruit of both the activity of God and the activity of the soul.

First, in what is called active prayer, God helps the soul in a way which allows it to keep the initiative and the principal share of activity in prayer. I choose to pray when I want to, and in the way I want to. My faculties are functioning in the ordinary way.

In a second stage, when God intervenes in prayer by a special grace, which becomes more and more powerful, he gradually affirms his sovereignty over the soul, which becomes more and more passive. We will see that this 'passivity' is the supreme activity of a human being ... This is what is called passive prayer.

St Teresa gives an illustration of this, which can help us to grasp the difference.

The Unitive Way
third passage, purification of spirit
Contemplation
Transforming union

The Illuminative Way
second passage, purification of senses
Mixed prayer
Prayer of simplicity

The Purgative Way
Conversion, the first passage
Active prayer

It seems to me that the garden may be watered in four different ways. Either the water must be drawn from a well, which is very laborious; or by a water-wheel and buckets, worked by a windlass – I have sometimes drawn it in this way, which is less laborious than the other, and brings up more water – or from a stream or spring, which waters the ground much better, for the soil then retains more moisture and needs watering less often, which entails far less work for the gardener; or by heavy rain, when the Lord waters it Himself without any labour of ours; and this is an incomparably better method than all the rest.

Now to apply these four methods of watering, by which this garden is to be maintained and without which it will fail. This is my purpose, and will, I think, enable me to explain something about the four stages of prayer, to which the Lord has, in His kindness, sometimes raised my soul.

. . . We may say that beginners in prayer are those who draw the water up out of the well; which is a great labour, as I have said. For they find it very tiring to keep the senses recollected, when they are used to a life of distraction . . . They should endeavour to meditate on the life of Christ, and thus the intellect will grow tired . . . This is what I mean by beginning to draw water from the well – and God grant there may be water in it!*

Here, the first way of watering the garden represents the active work of meditation. In the last three, the action of God becomes more and more preponderant.

CONVERSION

Let us not be in too much of a hurry. The first passage has got to be done properly: we are laying the foundations of all that is to follow. This is all the more true that, nowadays, for many people their entry into the monastic life represents a personal

Life, ch. XI.

conversion to Christ, or crowns such a conversion, from a more or less worldly way of life.

Conversion means turning your back on a certain way of living, a certain scale of values, and turning yourself towards God; it is an existential act of prayer. Conversion implies a considerable effort of ascesis, in order to establish, or re-establish the harmony of our being: submitting our passions to the order of reason, and opening our reason to the light of the Spirit. We learn how to situate ourselves in the presence of the Creator in our truth as creatures, as saved sinners in the presence of our Redeemer and the mercy of the gospel. It is a time of light and of obscurity – for it is all so beyond us that our eyes are weak. It is a time of struggle and of self-discovery, full of the joy of living in accordance with what we really are. There is a feeling of being in harmony with the universe, and a certain openness towards our brothers. It is springtime.

It often happens that the one who is converted has been seized by Christ and 'parachuted' for a while into an experience which is decisive on the spiritual level, but which is above his usual Christian 'tools'. His knowledge of doctrine is sadly lacking, or his human or moral structures are inadequate, or again perhaps he does not know how to make use of the Church's ways of expressing prayer. These gaps have to be filled by a slow and patient labour: when the Lord has caught him and carried him high up and away in the air, and has then set him down again on the ground. Converted, he will have to learn how to walk on his own feet.

Meditation, the slow assimilation and rumination of the articles of faith, is most necessary in order to establish his life of prayer on a solid basis. *Lectio divina* will be the privileged time for this.

LECTIO DIVINA

Our prayer life is based on the fact that God comes to us, he reveals himself to us in the book of life and of the universe, and in the Word which gives us the meaning of it. It is up to us to receive this Word, to let it dwell within us and transform us. What we call *lectio divina* is more than just a particular exercise: rather, it is a profound attitude which should impregnate all the activities in which we open our intelligence and our heart to God. So it englobes sacred studies, reading of the Bible and spiritual books, the readings made during the liturgy, etc.

The beginner needs solid and abundant nourishment. Most importantly, he must not confine himself to reasoning, but must open his heart wide to the love of the Lord. He should follow Guigue's method, and always let reading extend into meditation and prayer, and sometimes perhaps, contemplation.

Let us look now at the various forms that prayer can take. These are the degrees of so-called ordinary prayer:

1. Vocal prayer
2. Meditation
3. Affective mental prayer
4. Prayer of simple presence, or of simplicity

VOCAL PRAYER

When the disciples asked Christ to teach them how to pray, he answered: 'When you pray, say: Father . . . ' (Matthew 6:9–13; Luke 11:2–4). Jesus did not teach them some complicated technique of meditation (in the eastern sense), he passed on to them a prayer of petition: a prayer that is sublime in what it tells us of our relationship with the Father, and of what our attitude should be, but in the form of a simple vocal prayer.

So we are forbidden to underestimate this form of prayer. Most of the official prayers of the Church, the liturgy, are vocal prayer. Moreover, to whatever heights of prayer a Carthusian might rise, a preponderant part of his prayer will be given over, materially, to vocal prayer.

Every Our Father, every Hail Mary, and every psalm can be a religious act of great value, if I recite them in a spirit of faith, calmly and fully aware of the One to whom my words are addressed. One Our Father that has been well prayed is infinitely better than ten recited in a distracted way. We should never say prayers at top speed, just to have fulfilled an exterior obligation. A prayer that is only vocal, which is merely lip-service, is certainly not a true prayer. It deserves the Lord's reproach: 'When you are praying, do not heap up empty phrases as the Gentiles do; for they think that they will be heard because of their many words. Do not be like them, for your Father knows what you need before you ask him' (Matthew 6:7–8).

In their materiality, our prayers have no magical power over God. In them, we expose our needs in all simplicity to our Father who loves us and seeks our good (Luke 11:9–13).

But Jesus is not talking about repeated prayers, like the Hail Mary in the rosary, or monological prayers such as the Jesus Prayer: these are very simple means of keeping our attention fixed on God, and of remaining in a fundamental attitude towards him.

The recitation of the Brothers' Pater and Ave, for those who choose it, is a good example of vocal prayer sustaining effectively a profoundly simple and contemplative attitude of prayer during the long offices. St Teresa has already pointed out the fact that the highest graces of contemplation can be given during times of vocal prayer. Some minds, without this anchor, would be continually distracted and tossed about.

For the choir monks, the celebration of office, the official prayer of the Church, almost completely composed of texts of the Holy Scriptures, should be the channel and nourishment of their contemplation. Much depends on the more or less prayerful way in which it is celebrated: each of us has his share of responsibility for the atmosphere of unity, dignity and recollection which should reign there.

However, there certainly needs to be an initiation and a period of adaptation to this form of prayer. And some will have great difficulty in harmonising a simple interior attention to God with the succession of images and ideas that are inevitably proposed by the texts. Speaking of this, do not think that you have to pay attention to every idea and image. Cassian has already pointed out that it is very difficult to recite the psalms without distractions. This is particularly so for those whose prayer tends to be simple and direct, and for those young people who have been influenced by Eastern meditation.

But even for those whose prayer is usually silent, it can be useful, at times of fatigue or distractions in their personal prayer, to return to the slow recitation of a simple vocal prayer, especially that of the Our Father.

MEDITATION

Meditation is reflection on the truths of faith. We have seen the necessity of founding the spiritual life on a solid basis, personally assimilated. During the time of prayer we can use a book, and meditate, for example, on a text of the Scriptures;* or we can use a method, following a particular plan of reflection on any particular subject. There are many methods to choose from; the best are those that are the simplest.

As an example:

1. Choose a text or a subject.
2. Fix a time for the length of the prayer (e.g. half an hour).
3. Make the sign of the cross with great attention.
4. Place your body in a recollected attitude of prayer, expressing awareness of the presence of God; then take up a position which is alert, but can be kept without tension.
5. Make a deep act of faith in God present here and now in your heart.
6. Make a picture in your imagination of the subject chosen, followed by an intellectual consideration; then let your heart speak freely, and come to rest finally in a simple attention to the Lord.
7. End the time of prayer in thanksgiving to the Lord for the grace of this time spent with him, and renew the sign of the cross.

This is a simple use of our imagination, intelligence and heart. Abstract intellectual speculation is to be avoided, as well as excessive wordiness, or a hankering after sensory emotions.

---

*It can be helpful to read and study a text of the Bible at night, with commentary etc., if necessary, and then pray on it more spontaneously the following morning.

There must always be times of silence at the end, when God can speak to us if he so wishes, and when the Spirit can move us towards his wisdom and love. Even in meditation, we have to remember that the Spirit is present and active within us, and that true contact with God takes place on the level of faith and love.

AFFECTIVE PRAYER

With time, quite naturally, there is an imperceptible transition, and the part of reflection diminishes. We have looked at all the most important questions, and gone back many times over the same subjects: a rapid glance or so is enough to evoke a whole host of ideas, without having to look at them again explicitly and in detail – a word, or a text, suffices to bring back a general remembrance of them.

The heart, too, is more awake and instructed. It is more easily kindled and is increasingly to the fore in prayer. Prayer now becomes what is called mental prayer, defined by St Teresa as 'a friendly intercourse and frequent solitary conversation with Him who, as we know, loves us'.*

It is an interior, familiar conversation of the soul with the Lord, about everything and anything of concern, our desires and troubles, our life, joys, our love and trust; all shared spontaneously, in simple, personal words. Sometimes there will be a need to be silent, in the joy of the intimate, peaceful presence of the Friend; sometimes we will feel the Lord absent, often in the awareness of a fault, past or present; we will cry out to him with tears.

This prayer has greater power to transform us and make us better than prayer of a more intellectual type. It reaches to the heart, and it is the heart that makes us act.

Sometimes there will be intense and overwhelming emotions, particularly in passionate natures, but their authenticity will have to be proved by conversion of the way we live, in concrete acts. Moreover, seeking after sensory emotions can turn into

---

*Life, ch. VIII.

self-seeking. We must avoid stirring up our more outward emotions in an excessive way; our sensitivity itself has to be refined, and become more spiritual. Our heart too has a need to listen, and to be in silence: a need of deep peace.

But we must be firmly convinced that the most important fruit of the labour of our imagination and intelligence is in prayer of the heart. We must not give priority to the former over the latter. It is love that unites us to God, and allows us to know him in truth. Prayer of the heart is the most direct path to contemplation.

19

The Prayer of Simplicity

Our efforts to live a life of prayer, sustained by grace, normally lead to one of the various forms of the prayer of simplicity. We can see the different variations of this kind of prayer in the variety of names that authors give it, depending on which aspect of it they want to stress: prayer of the heart, prayer of simple presence; prayer of simple surrender to God, active recollection, rest, silence, quietude, acquired contemplation (all described as 'active', as opposed to passive or mystical recollection, rest, etc.).

It is a real grace of mental prayer, but is not, strictly speaking, mystical prayer. It is within reach of the efforts of our intelligence, and is the furthest we can go to prepare ourselves to receive the grace of infused contemplation. That is why it is so extremely important for us. We are going to take a very close look at it.

This prayer does not drop down from heaven as from outer space. Nature does not have to jump up a level. It is the mature fruit of the pattern of evolution in prayer that we have already observed. We could describe this evolution as a gradual simplification and concentration of the faculties of intelligence, imagination and will, which lead finally to an attention that is intuitive, englobing, charged with love, and fixed more or less constantly, although obscurely, on God and on his presence; it is accompanied by a peaceful abandon of oneself to the Lord.

The faculties do not come to a complete standstill, except for very short moments, but their rhythm and importance are much reduced. Discursive activity is at a minimum, and the heart is filled with a few profound sentiments, that are like waves moving in the depths, rather than the rufflings of a moving surface.

This is not the effect of an act of authority imposed by the will in order to conform to some theory about prayer. Of course, a lot does depend on us. We are in surroundings which are favourable to recollection, with an absence of disturbance or provocation of our faculties: that is, with exterior and interior silence. Attention to an invisible Person is like a delicate plant that we have to cultivate and protect against all the seductions of material objects. And we have to invest the necessary time and effort into it. But if all these conditions are fulfilled, this prayer, and this contemplation, follow on quite naturally.

It is not a violent state. We are very close to nature here, and there are plenty of natural analogies. The intellectual, who has spent a long time on the discursive work of analysis, sits back with deep satisfaction in the simple view of the truth at last procured in synthesis. The artist, seized with admiration at the sight of a magnificent landscape, takes it in, in an act of general, englobing contemplation. The heart of a lover is filled with the love and the diffuse presence of the one he loves. The mother of a sick child will have that concern ever present in her heart, dominating all other feelings.

As you can see, the activities of the intelligence and of the heart are intimately linked. It is love that provokes the search, and focuses the attention. Love is nourished by the view of its object, and takes pleasure in it. The heart rejoices in union with the beloved.

This is all the more true in the domain of prayer, as the realities of faith remain invisible. The intelligence is always standing at a distance, and only the heart, borne on the wings of faith, can go beyond the finite limits of conceptual knowledge to reach God as he really is. The heart of the lover can know the one he loves, more deeply than what he can say of him. Love is source of experiential knowledge, obscure and non-conceptual, but real.

There are two important consequences to this: (1) the aim of prayer is not to have profound thoughts about God; (2) so the essential is not to have many thoughts, but to have much love.

FOSTERING THIS PRAYER

In her advice on how to enter into the prayer of simplicity, St Teresa of Avila insists on these two points. The most important practice by which we can foster it is the recollection of all the powers of our soul, and entry into ourselves to live in the company of Jesus who is there.

It is in the depths of the heart that contemplation takes place, there where God, One and Trine, communicates himself by the gift of grace. In prayer, it is very important that we should be turned in this direction.

THE PRACTICE OF THE PRESENCE OF GOD

This requires an energetic and constant effort of recollection. It is not easy to be always attentive to the presence of God. Particularly in the beginning, there has to be a struggle, an alert and vigilant guard of our faculties against their tendency to wander around, attracted by anything that glitters: this is especially true of our imagination and memory.

The solitary has to learn how to live physically within the four walls of his cell, and, above all, in the reality of the present moment. But the present must become presence: presence to oneself in order to welcome the One who dwells in our hearts.

This presence is an object of faith for us. To make it become more alive, we can use the resources of our intelligence, our imagination and our love. Each one will be drawn to finding his own means of doing this. It could be, for example, that the remembrance or rumination of a text of the sacred Scriptures helps us, or an icon, the rosary, the Jesus Prayer, various ejaculatory prayers, etc.

Moreover, all that we see or hear, every person, every object, can become a reminder of the Creator, of his beauty and mercy. We have the special privilege of surroundings that have been designed precisely in order to be a sign of God.

But without a doubt, the most efficient means is the interior dialogue with Jesus, simply sharing with him our hopes and fears, our joys and sorrows, from day to day. He is our companion* on the way, he can see deep within us, and is the only one who knows us through and through. And, portrayed in a human face, his presence is the presence of infinite love, gazing upon us. In the sanctuary of our heart, he is there, waiting for us. One look, one second, suffices to meet him in the reciprocity of a simple, profound friendship.

Just a simple turning of the will towards God, a movement of the heart instantly leaping up to God, like a spark from the coal: we are always capable of that, and it is something which binds us powerfully and gently to the Lord.

This is the great monastic tradition of the prayer of the heart. The backdrop of our conscience should be woven of these short, ardent prayers which unite us to God in our heart, and which are there ready to surge up at any time. It is a habit we have to cultivate with great care, and which quickly becomes a second nature.

For those who are attracted to it, the 'Jesus Prayer' (one form of prayer of the heart) is a good way of maintaining an awareness of the presence of God throughout the day. It helps us to grow towards the prayer of simplicity too, during our times of mental prayer. It gives our discursive faculties what they need in order to be focused (without actually setting off a movement of discourse). It is a prayer addressed to the person of Jesus, and comes from the heart.

Personally I prefer the age-old custom of simply invoking the name of Jesus (or Lord Jesus). But the formula in use actually – 'Lord Jesus Christ, Son of God, have mercy on me a sinner (or: on us sinners)' – may be better suited to more active minds. And there is a variety of graces: some will be happier with formulae such as 'Father', 'Come, Holy Spirit', 'Mary', for example. Regarding our subject, the important thing is that the prayer should be short (the best would be just one syllable) and ardent – a spark from the heart – and, preferably, addressed to a person.

---

*It is better to avoid letting the imagination become too 'theatrical' in this, as it can sometimes be childish. This is something that pertains to the domain of faith and of spiritual realities.

DIFFICULTIES

And so we come to the problem of distractions. As the role played by the heart increases, and the activity of the imagination and the discursive intelligence is simplified, the latter tend to become bored, and set out to find something more substantial to do. We have to be very patient with these somewhat narrow-minded servants, and not pay much attention to their senseless ramblings; when we become aware that they are off-track, we have to bring them back gently but firmly to their task, which is attention to God. Sometimes, the whole time of prayer will be spent on 'coming back' . . . but be patient, it is a good prayer, which continually reaffirms the heart's choice. It will bear fruit later or in other things.

We need a lot of perseverance in order to advance along the path of prayer. It will soon look as though simplicity and silence are useless. We want efficiency and visible success. It isn't easy to persevere in a prayer of simplicity when our faculties are rebelling against the monotonous food that is offered to them, and we need strength and love to do so.

For we have to remember that this kind of prayer is not always pleasant. It can be arid and testing, with an acute awareness of the infinite distance which separates us from God, tears of remorse, an excruciating consciousness of our inability to love, or even to believe . . .

ADVANTAGES AND DISADVANTAGES

On a lighter note, I have jotted down a few traits of character or culture which can be more or less an advantage with regard to entry into the prayer of simplicity, and so to contemplation. These are simply predispositions which are more or less favourable, and not absolute obstacles. God's grace is all-powerful, and sometimes seems that it is precisely in our natural weakness that the Lord wants to manifest his power.

ADVANTAGES	DISADVANTAGES
Lack of imagination and memory.	Imagination and discursive faculty very developed. A memory packed full of images and ideas.
Discourse difficult.	Easy discourse.
The whole of one's being in simple and immediate contact with reality.	Intellectualism: transposition of everything into rational ideas and tendency to reduce reality to what can be grasped by thought.
Great faith.	Need to prove everything.
Affective, warm-hearted nature.	A cold or inhibited nature.
The dimension of 'being' is predominant.	
Capacity to give and receive.	Hyperactivity and restlessness, tending towards doing and efficiency.
A sense of gratuity.	
Being a woman, generally.	Aestheticism (?).

We can see a reversal of values very much in line with the gospel: blessed are the poor! Here, people who are gifted in ways that bring success in an active life – active in a worldly sense, at least – are at a disadvantage. Unless they renounce their riches, they cannot enter the Kingdom of God. Remember: our aim is contemplation, in which God himself is the principal agent. Our activity must gradually give way to the action of the Spirit. To the extent that we hang on to our activity (and this is often in proportion to our natural aptitudes, and the pleasure we draw from exercising them), and to our 'lights', so also do we risk obstructing and refusing the disconcerting and, to a certain degree, impoverishing light of the Spirit. The challenge made by Christ to the rich young man is addressed to each of us.

Prayer is openness to reality, openness of our whole person to the unpredictable gift of all that is real. Our ideas are merely transfer copies of a part of what is real, seen from a certain angle. Wanting to enclose God in our ideas is like trying to enclose him in a poor caricature of ourselves.

Prayer is the respiration of faith. Faith, precisely, is willing to take the risk of going beyond what can be verified. We are always confronted with the same challenge to go out of ourselves and our poor limits, towards the unknown horizons of Love.

A heart that is inclined to love, will love. This is a great gift, and already the fruit of much love.

The place of contemplative prayer is the domain of one who loves. Its feast is the gift freely given: ultimately, the gift of receptivity.

Women, in the make-up of their being, and their psychology, are people of prayer. This is true of men too, when they are men of heart, and know how to live with their whole being. Women are often able to dwell a long time on a few ideas or basic sentiments with little discursive activity. Mary pondered on all these things in her heart.

There is a delicate problem regarding the case of the aesthete. Insomuch as he is gifted with so-called 'feminine' qualities – sensitivity, attention to concrete reality, and a certain receptivity to the beauty of beings – he has the same advantages as a woman. But this is often counterbalanced in men by a stronger tendency to want to produce something (exteriorly), and by temptations of attachment on the level of the senses, which is, basically, the domain of forms. It is doubly difficult for him to attain to what is purely spiritual, and to go beyond the domain of forms. I think a lot depends in this matter on the kind of aesthetic sensitivity involved (painting, poetry, music, etc.), and on the strength of the inner calling. For the poet, at least, the ultimate exigencies of his charisma can lead him to transcend discourse. But I am not claiming to give the last word on this subject; only to say that, to me at least, it seems that too little attention has been paid to it as yet.

The state of the prayer of simplicity is a great grace and is the effect of a great love of God. If it is not God's will to give someone the grace of mystical prayer in a way that is habitual, the soul can find sanctity in this state: a sanctity that is all the more authentic since it is simple and hidden. I say 'in a way that is habitual', because there will almost certainly be moments of mystical prayer in such a life, although not frequent enough to constitute a state.

20

Union of Will

Now we are going to enter into the sphere of the intimate union of the soul with God. This union is realised with growing intensity in the phases of what are called simple union (or union of the will), ecstatic union, and transforming union. Let us first take an overall view of these different types of mystical union, and try to draw out the general movement of it starting at God's first brief, fleeting hold over the soul; passing through the ultimate purification of the night of the spirit, and the powerful rapture of ecstasy; and coming to the permanent and totally transparent union of the soul, plunged in the life of the Holy Trinity, and yet perfectly free with regard to the exterior world. This is the supreme triumph of Love in the heart of a human being, and the plenitude of the life of Christ within him or her. The Spirit takes flesh in our humanity, in the whole of our humanity, in order to transform it and give it a new life, illuminated by the inaccessible Light of the Father.

For those who receive, or will receive mystical graces, or who will have to accompany those who receive them, it is useful to know something of the classical spiritual journey – although the individual variations are innumerable. The testimony of the mystics will also be an inspiration to those who are following, and who will follow, more hidden ways, for it brings up to the level of consciousness the treasures of the life of grace that all carry within themselves. Moreover, the phenomena associated with mystical experience are an outward expression of spiritual realities, which thus become more palpable to us who are walking in faith; I am not referring to the accessory and more spectacular phenomena, like levitation, etc., but to the more essential ones, such as interior absorption, the divine hold over the faculties of the soul, the dazzled admiration of ecstasy, and the harmonious compenetration of the human by the divine in the ultimate transformation.

THE MYSTICAL GRACE OF SIMPLE UNION OF WILL WITH GOD

There is a union of God with the essence of the soul.

This union is obscure, but with absolute certitude that God is in the soul.

Often there is suspension of the faculties of the soul – intelligence, memory, will.

The senses are capable of acting, but with difficulty (moving around, coming out of prayer). When fully operative, it is of short duration (half an hour), with differing degrees of intensity before returning to quietude.

Outside the specific time of prayer, there is an awareness of the presence of God, perceived more or less clearly.

Effects:

A lasting state of union with God, particularly union of the will.

A contact with God-who-is-Love which transforms and kindles the heart, and is a source of strength and courage to give oneself for the glory of God (sacrifice, prayer, work).

Death to the world, detachment, freedom.

Complete abandon into the hands of the Father.

The will is totally in harmony with the will of God.

Effective and practical love of one's neighbour.

Love of the Church, sorrow to see that God is not loved as he should be.

A state that is not definitive: the devil does his utmost to destroy it.

These, then, are the effects of the grace of mystical union. It is a very special grace which, in God's wisdom, is not given to many. Sometimes it is given in view of a role to be played in the Church; and it seems that sometimes it is given just for God's own pleasure alone. But the state to which it leads the

soul is the desire of every person touched by the love of God
and stirred by the example of Christ. Each one of the saints
has attained to it, but not all by the same path of mystical
grace. The perfection of charity is the aim of every monk.
Mystical grace is a short cut to that. As such, we can desire
it, and make ourselves ready to receive it, insofar as we are
able.

THE WAY OF ORDINARY GRACE

If we do not receive the mystical grace of union, we are not for
that excluded from the state of union. Simply, we follow a more
'ordinary' way, the way of ordinary grace, more hidden and
more humble, more difficult and long, although no less
demanding, for the aim is the same: that our will should be
totally united with the will of God, our heart plunged into the
heart of God in a union in which they become one heart, one
sole Love. The Lord wants our whole heart, he does not want
us to keep back anything at all, however big or small. Depending
on how complete our gift is, God's gifts will be more or less
lavish.

We have to understand this fundamental truth: union with
God, whether by the means of mystical grace or by the way of
ordinary grace, is, in essence, the union of our will with the
will of God. So it is a union of love, but of love translated into
acts.

ILLUSIONS

We are capable of many illusions in this matter. We think that
we are united to the will of God, when in fact we are far from
it. For example, we take our desires to be the reality, our
velleities for the expression of the depth of our will. St Teresa
observes rather mischievously:

> I smile sometimes to see certain souls who, when they are
> at prayer, imagine that they are willing to be humiliated
> and publicly insulted for the love of God, and later they

are seen trying, if possible, to hide some slight fault, or if they are not guilty, and are charged with it, God help us!*

A man of prayer has got to be very, very realistic. All the more so, as he is plunging into an interior world in which the boundaries between the imaginary and the real are easily blurred, and where he risks being, not with the Lord, but alone with himself. He has to be very careful to transpose his love into exterior acts.

A more subtle illusion is conformity to the will of God in events, even in sorrows such as the death of a loved one, but through human wisdom, which in itself is in fact a good thing: unable to control these evils, it makes a virtue of necessity. We have here a wise resignation, and not a love that embraces wholeheartedly the will of God. God's will must be willed.

And how many of our prayers could be summed up in the phrase: 'My will be done on earth and in heaven'?

Establishing the order of true charity within ourselves is not the work of a day. In the mystical grace of union we can see the form of the spiritual reality to which we are tending: all the faculties of the soul are absorbed in the silence of God, whilst the soul, in its depths, receives the direct imprint of Love, and becomes fire itself.

THE WAY OF INCARNATE LOVE

I do as the Father has commanded me
so that the world may know that I love my Father.
(John 14:31)

The end is Love, the way is love: a love made flesh in real life, for the Way is Christ. It is by practising love that we learn how to love. Love is nurtured by concrete acts, by real things, for there is nothing more real than Love. Freedom and detachment are fruits of love. If love is genuine, all the rest will follow. Moreover, for us, our whole rule of life is aimed at directing our faculties towards God, and preventing their dispersion to

---

Fifth Mansion, ch. 3.

secondary aims. This makes us all the more free to consecrate ourselves to loving God, and the whole of his creation.

The touchstone is, of course, love of our neighbour: love of our brother, of our fellow human beings, compassion, refusal to judge, unconditional welcome, thoughtful and effective love. Love gives, or is non-existent.

When we exercise love, we have to beware intensity of feeling, especially when it is accompanied by a greedy pursuit, which only wants to take hold of God in sensory gratification and consolation. Union with God resides in the will, and not in our sensual faculties.

True love grows through acts: acts accomplished for God (prayer, adoration, etc.) and for our brothers. There is an important spiritual law here that we have to remember. It is only acts which use the whole potential of virtue already acquired – called, because of this, 'intense' acts – which will further develop that virtue; on the contrary, 'weak' acts, good in themselves, but which do not exercise all the charity acquired, risk diminishing its strength. This is a theological truth of considerable practical consequence. Someone who is not advancing, is retrograding. It must be said that intensity means perfection of the act itself and purity of intention, and not necessarily effort or violence in making it.

One person goes ahead, doing his duty, simply, without fervour, as also with no apparent lapses; his acts are good but weak, and he makes no progress. Someone else may appear much the same exteriorly, but his love is awake, and is strengthening him to be faithful and careful to purify his attention, and so add to his acts that little something which makes them good and intense. He makes constant progress, and one day, with the help of God's grace, will reach union of will. Let us always aim at quality in our acts of love, trying to live on a level of the grace we have received; let us not bury our talent in the ground of lazy mediocrity. At the Charterhouse, it is an advantage to be a downright sinner: who has no inclination to good, and has to wage a constant war against his evil tendencies. You either advance, or you drown. Praised be God for his mercy and wisdom!

In any case, let us never neglect an opportunity to love, and enter thus into the heart of the Lord in this union of will, without which there is no mystical union or true religion. This is the foundation of the whole edifice of life in God.

I delight to do your will, O my God; your law is within my heart. (Psalm 39:8)

21

The Night of the Spirit

THE FIRE OF SACRIFICE

The Lord comes down in fire, the fire of an ardent love that wants to purify us and adapt us to himself, so that union may be possible. To be united to God, we have to be like him, we have to become fire.

We have looked at the first passage which tears us away from the world to turn us to God; and the second passage which purifies our sensitivity, and adapts it to the spirit. Now we come to the third passage, the third actualisation of the paschal mystery of Christ in us, in which our spirit is to be purified and adapted to God.

In the previous conference, we saw that this passage takes place between simple union and ecstatic union. It is then that it is usually at its most intense, but in actual fact it is present as soon as there is mystical prayer: so, in a way, it is already present in the prayer of quietude, but particularly from the prayer of union onwards, until the transformation of the soul is fully accomplished, in transforming union. The reason is simple: it is the very light of contemplation which is the fire that purifies and transforms. The night of the spirit is the reverse side of the intimate communication of God, and is concomitant with it. The invasion of the soul by God is a source of unspeakable joy, but source also of suffering and of painful separations. Why?

THE SOUL'S INAPTITUDE FOR UNION

There are two causes: the elevation of Divine Wisdom, and the inaptitude and impurity of the soul. In relation to God, our created being is nothing, our heart is ridiculously narrow, and our intelligence is weak and tiny. When God begins to communicate himself, not through the mediation of words and images, but directly, essence to essence, as happens already in the grace of union, this is so far beyond the light we are used to that it is as darkness to our blinded intelligence. It is like an owl blinded by the sun.

Contemplation operates a profound psychological change, and the psychological habits of our mind resist this invasion. The soul was directed towards the exterior, from where its food came, by the windows of the senses. The intelligence and the will operated according to the laws of human activity; they moved according to the attraction of their particular object, presented by the senses and the other faculties. From now on, they are to be subjected to the motion of God which comes to them not from the exterior, but from the interior, from the very depths of the soul.

The attention of the soul is now to be captivated by this spring of living water gushing up within it, and filling it with love and light, without any contribution of the faculties. These, like the senses, will only receive from the overflowing life of the Spirit.

The resistance of the faculties to this change is the first obstacle to the adaptation of the spirit to God. It is also the first cause of the sufferings of this night. Resistance is all the stronger when the usual ways of acting are too intellectual, or are possessed as riches, as that which gives value to the individual. It is not easy to let go of them, but there is so much to gain from doing so, even on the psychological level: the activity of the soul is immediately freed from any psychological and moral disturbances which have their root in the way these faculties operate.

IMPURITY OF THE SOUL

Then there is the impurity of the soul. We are speaking of a soul that has already undergone the purification of the senses. It has received graces of passive prayer. It has a profound love

of God, and we saw how much good could be said of it
regarding its virtue. And yet, in the new light of God, this soul
is seen to be impure. The life of the senses has been put in
order, but the roots of disorder still remain more or less intact
in the soul, in the form of deep tendencies that have hitherto
been hidden to it. As well as that, there are the actual imperfections of such a soul: coming mostly from a misuse of spiritual
gifts already received. The chief faults are pride and presumption, and a 'carnal' understanding of spiritual things. How
pleased they are with themselves, the poor things, and what
scales they have on their eyes!

The soul is the battlefield where two contraries, divine action
and human action, the purity of God and the impurity of
humanity, are going to fight it out. And the devil, with all his
perfidy, is going to stand guard over this passage, in order to
prevent it at all cost.

And we must not hide the fact: this passage is infinitely more
painful and terrifying than the previous one. It is a matter of
life or death for the spirit. We are going to have to see the love
of God in the face of Jesus, agonising to the point of death,
mocked, and abandoned by God. So let us enter the garden,
and go up to the place of the Skull. Our humanity is there
waiting for us, and our truth . . . and our Father. Christ
descended into Sheol for us.

THE INTERIOR SUFFERINGS OF THE NIGHT

These differ for each individual, according to the imperfections
that have to be purified, and according to God's plan for each
one. We may be tempted to think that the mystics are exaggera-
ting when they speak of the night, oppressive weight, paralysing
darkness, suffocating anguish, an abyss of unspeakable suffering, the abandon and enmity of God . . . There are moments
of remission, and of light; but these do not last long . . .
However, the love of God is always burning in the depths of
the soul, with a very obscure, undefinable sentiment that the
Lord is present. Already in this life the soul is undergoing its
purgatory; it is not hell, but for the soul in the throes of this

suffering it may well seem like it. It is in fact the soul's love – its desire to love, and the feeling that it is forever separated from the object of its love – that is torturing it.

Note that the night of the spirit consists essentially in the interior sufferings caused directly by the communication of divine light to the essence of the soul. There, God is at work without any intermediary, and with no preliminary co-operation from the faculties, whose only activity is to assume the effects of his work. The exterior sufferings, of which we will say a word, are either the secondary effects of interior grace, or the action of God, received through the instruments of people and events. They can be very intense, but their effect upon us depends on the way we live them and co-operate with them.

EXTERIOR SUFFERINGS

The interior trial produces psychological effects: fear, fatigue, confusion, varying degrees of incapacity for intellectual work, memory blanks, etc. Prayer is often impossible, and the soul no longer has the overall attention to God which it retained, so preciously, in the previous trials.

Sometimes there can be disturbances on the physical level of sensory activity: mysterious 'psychosomatic' illnesses; and in some cases of extraordinary mystical phenomena, such as ecstasy, levitation, stigmata, etc., the body is subject to real violence.

There are also trials that come through our neighbour: criticisms, calumnies, opposition to our projects. The tempter, of course, makes the most of these. The proximity of the Lord always attracts opposition ('the servant is not above his master'), and so do the imperfections of a soul which, although closely united to God by union of the will and deeply engaged in his service, is not yet completely purified; in the eyes of the 'virtuous', these imperfections, and a certain lack of virtue, seem to be incompatible with graces of such elevation.

A SLOWER PACE

We have been describing this night at its greatest intensity. It can last for months, for years. Sometimes, however, it can be intermittent, and interrupted by long periods of rest. Also the trials can vary in intensity in different persons. Don't forget that it is a short cut. The same work of adaptation and purification can be done in more ordinary ways, although more slowly, and generally never finished in this life. A life spent seeking God, spent in his presence, contemplating the face of God and the face of humanity in the Word of God, will develop a sense of God and a knowledge of self in a very real though imperceptible way, and will tend towards the same result as the mystical night. The Lord knows how to make use of second causes as well – the people and events in our lives – in order to open us up to his love. He is so good at hiding his action in everyday things that nobody notices it – and it is all the more efficacious.

PSYCHIC PHENOMENA AND MENTAL DISTURBANCES

The psychological effects of this night can be similar to the psychic disturbances of illnesses (for example, cyclothymia, melancholy). In both cases, the clinical charts are sometimes quite similar. There is no reason to be scandalized about this. On a sensory level, a person has no two ways of reacting to shock: the sensory reaction to the violence of it does not take into account whatever may be the cause of it. So it is not surprising that the perturbations produced by the strength of the action of God in this night are similar to certain psychopathological disturbances with other causes.

In any case, we have to admit that our poor human nature is very prone to pathological tendencies, and that these are now a part of the consequences of original sin. Hardly any one of us is exempt from them. These tendencies are present at varying degrees, in a benign state most of the time, and more or less concealed from ourselves if not from others, in our ordinary everyday habits, in interior inhibitions or fixations, and in the compensations we seek or demand from those around us. Thus each of us adapts his life to the exigencies of his tendencies (for example, tendencies to obsession, melancholy, depressive mood-swings,* excessive affective demands, a certain incapacity for intimate relationships, etc.), and obtains right of city for them, by more or less peaceful means (!) in his milieu. Our community life is made up of these reciprocal adjustments of which we are often not even conscious, so imperative are they, and so much a part of our habits, until the divine light of this night uncovers their fallacious harmony.

> Fire, when applied to wood, first dehumidifies it, dispelling all moisture and making it give off any water it contains. Then it gradually turns the wood black, makes it dark and ugly, and even causes it to emit a bad odour. By drying out the wood, the fire brings to light and expels all those ugly and dark accidents which are contrary to fire . . .
>
> Similarly, we should philosophize about this divine, loving fire of contemplation. Before transforming the soul, it purges it of all contrary qualities. It produces a blackness and darkness and brings to the fore the soul's ugliness; thus the soul seems worse than before and unsightly and abominable. The divine purge stirs up all the foul and vicious humours of which the soul was never before aware; never did it realize there was so much evil in itself, since these humours were so deeply rooted.†

Under the purifying action of the light of God, our hidden tendencies come up to the surface in their black nudity, until we become painfully aware of them.‡ In the night of the spirit – and, for us, solitude increases the pressure by eliminating all derivatives – these tendencies are brought to their maximum intensity. They greatly influence the soul's reaction to the action

---

*The mood-swings of the cyclothymic are more or less excessive, going from low to high.
†John of the Cross, *Dark Night*, Book II, ch. 10, 1.2.
‡Ancient authors have spoken about the influence of melancholy on contemplative aridity and sexual temptations.

of God, and so appear to the psychiatrist to give signs justifying the diagnosis of a pathological condition, with the well-known characteristics of obsession, melancholy, and manic-depression.

DISCERNMENT

In spite of these similarities and their interpenetration, the troubles caused by the night of the spirit can usually be distinguished from psychological disorders.

In some cases there is no direct action of God, but only psychiatric illness (for example, paranoia with religious delirium, or an attack of schizophrenia). The person thinks and says himself to be undergoing a mystical experience; but the psychotic character of the experience can normally be seen in a certain degradation of personal and moral behaviour, or by something strange, exaggerated or unseemly in claims made by the person, or in his acts. The absence of true humility is often noticed. In this discernment it is useful to have some knowledge of the clinical signs of psychosis, and medical expertise may be needed.

Mixed cases are a much more delicate matter: the cause of the disorders is mystical, that is, due to an authentic communication of divine light, but it is received into a subject affected by pathological tendencies. A hasty judgement could have harmful consequences.

Above all, it is the behaviour of the person and his progress, assessed not on the violence of the attacks nor on their frequency, but on general criteria observed over a length of time, which will enable one to discern the predominant influence which will finally take over: the action of grace, or the psychosis (or neurosis).

Normally, psychological illness impoverishes the mind and personality to some extent, because of the stagnations, aberrations, and the amount of psychic energy expended on the interior conflicts and defence mechanisms it produces. It tends to constrict attitudes, both towards oneself – closing the sufferer upon himself in an arrogant or anxious way – and towards others and the world, through a lack of contact with exterior reality, and of adaptation to others. The ability to love is often weakened.

On the contrary, with time, the night of the spirit bears fruits of life and light. Even on a psychological level, it can be seen as enriching the personality, with consistent daily victories gained in the most difficult circumstances, and an extraordinary deepening of the ability to love and forgive: a radical move away from oneself as centre in order to open up to an infinitely vaster world, a source of truth and humility, fruitful in creative activities. The personality emerges from it greatly strengthened and enriched.

The battle between the Spirit and illness will often be a long one, with victories and defeats on both sides in equal measure, and no signs as to how it is going to end. Much patience is needed, as this can last for years. No one can really know exactly what is happening in this obscure confrontation between grace and liberty, the devil and Christ – the soul in its ultimate secret, and God.

THE OUTCOME

Medicine can be of help to a certain extent (and we must not look down on it), by trying to neutralize the effects of the illness and support the psyche, but in the end, the real drama is beyond its competence. Here, only the Spirit can heal. Our part is to go beyond the sensory, psychological level, beyond the rational level even, by constantly surrendering ourselves to the Lord, in an attitude of trust and abandon, an attitude of faith, in spite of the total darkness surrounding us. God alone is the health of the soul.

The final outcome could be one of several possibilities.

Sometimes, the pathological tendency gives way under the action of the night, and disappears, leaving the soul transparent to the Spirit of God. In this case, it seems that the suffering has been increased and the trial prolonged by the pathological tendencies, but that, in the end, they have been the means of progress, by forcing a deeper descent into oneself in order to assume them, and into Christ in order to surmount them, in a more complete poverty and abandon.

Sometimes the pathological tendencies do not give way under the action of the night. They may even develop under its influence, and become more tyrannical. This can be a sign of failure and, in this case, leads to generalised spiritual degradation.

But this is not always the case. The ways of the Lord are not our ways. The One who said to Paul, 'My grace is sufficient for you, for power is made perfect in weakness' (2 Corinthians 12:9), may choose not to heal a pathological tendency in someone in whom, nevertheless, the Spirit reigns, and who is living a genuine mystical grace. We find neurotic, even psychotic streaks in some of the saints. The answer lies perhaps in the utility for the Church of more than one way of purification.

The pathological tendency can disturb contact with reality, and the exterior expression of an act which is nevertheless pure in its spiritual source. To the extent that a person is conscious and free, he can freely will good, and bring it about, as he sees it (that is, in a distorted way perhaps, but not entirely obscured).

The Lord can leave one of his friends with some very real psychic handicap, which causes humiliation and suffering, but which can also be a source of sanctity, and of a greater ability to love and have compassion. In our modern world, with all its tensions and contradictions, this is perhaps one of the commonest ways of sharing in the sufferings of Christ. In any case, let us at least take the resolution never to judge or despise anyone who has to bear this burden – perhaps for you or me? He too is Christ among us: '*you did it to me*' (Matthew 25:40).

When the organ of our superior faculties, the cerebral substance, is destroyed, there is no possibility of a spiritual act being grafted onto the activity of the intelligence and the will. Apart from this case, even in the gravest psychoses, the lesions will most often be only partial, and there will be at least intervals of lucidity. In some cases, a state of dementia, for example, can have been accepted in advance, before the person succumbs to it (for instance, the father of St Thérèse of Lisieux). Moreover we can never be completely sure of the degree of lucidity and liberty still remaining in someone who is mentally ill. In any case, God loves that person just as much as another who is in good health, and he can give him graces that are genuinely mystical – to the extent that he needs them, perhaps? (as in the case of Père Surin, where folly and a true mystical life seem to have co-existed). The region of our souls where mystical grace is received is beyond the realm of our faculties: it remains inviolable, and is always accessible to God.

God sometimes gives us the consolation of being able to see and experience holiness even here in this life. There are also other kinds of sanctity that are reserved for his own knowledge and joy alone, in this world. There will be surprises on the day of judgement, when the last will be shown to be first.

Essential Love is not subject to observation. Its most beautiful triumphs are disguised beneath the thickest veil of mysterious and often painful darkness. This is how the love of Christ triumphed, and how the light of the resurrection appeared shining through the morning mist.

22

The Effects of the Night

The night purifies the soul and prepares it to be united to God. As it is chiefly through the theological virtues of faith, hope and charity that we are united immediately to God, it is particularly in these virtues that we see the effects of the night.

THE NIGHT OF FAITH

Faith relies on the Word of God; its belief is based on the sole authority of the One who is speaking.

In fact, our faith relies also on a number of things of a more human order: the authority of those who taught us, cultural and social habits, our human understanding, the rational constructions in which it has been elaborated, what we think we understand of it, etc. We live very comfortably, very much at home, in the house of our faith, and we look with pity, if not with contempt, on those who do not have the same light; until the day comes when the Lord takes this light, this too human security, away from us. We become aware of the impenetrable darkness that the object of our faith is for our intelligence, we see ourselves hanging over a bottomless abyss, with nothing else to hold on to but the fine thread of this stark act of our adhesion to God's Word. We understand nothing, we feel nothing, we simply believe. Why? The reason? Simply that we believe. There is, hidden in this act, most surely, a love that is hidden even to itself. We ourselves are only conscious of plodding on, plodding on in the night . . . and for such a length of time; whilst, almost unknown to us, our faith is slowly transformed, until the day dawns when the darkness of faith, still just as opaque, becomes the light of our heart. That which no one has ever seen, that which is beyond all that the heart of a human being can imagine, becomes the pillars which uphold our world: it is there, and 'real'. We wake up, and – no wonder – the sun is shining, the sky is above us, and the earth beneath our feet. Everything is just as it has always been. But we had gone away. Now, we are back. Where? Here, everywhere.

The contemplative has to 'lose the faith' one day (the faith as something possessed, materialized) in order to find it. Only a faith that has been purified in this way gives access to the true God. All 'our' gods, however sublime, however orthodox, however much in line with the thought of great theologians, or with the Bible itself, are but straw, to be burnt in the dark fire of a love that wants the One, the only One, who is. God gives no guarantees, and he is guaranteed by nothing: our insurance god, our stand-in god, the big policeman, the meter of justice, the substitute for father, mother, lover, Beauty, truth, and being itself, is but an idol if he has not surged from the dark flames of mystery.

There are philosophers who tell us that our ideas of God are contradictory. Rather, they are like nuts: you have to crack the hard shell of the words in order to extract what they contain. They are stars in the night.

This only appears to be negative. It is in fact the passage from the level of words that signify to the level of the realities signified. John of the Cross speaks of the eyes we are seeking, and which are inscribed on our hearts. During this night we become aware of the substantial light placed within us by faith. First we have to give up trying to circumscribe with our words he who is 'un-circumscribable' – how tired we get of words! Then he who can be circumscribed by nothing can give himself in all gratuity, in amazing simplicity. It is from within that the Word comes; in the silence he pronounces substantial words, which not only signify reality and life, but which are the substance of them. Within us, the Father gives himself in his Word, the Spirit unites them in Love; by the Spirit, the risen Christ communicates his life and his love to us; humanity becomes the Body of Christ, creation sings the glory of the Father, for eternity.

THE NIGHT OF HOPE

The heart that has been touched by God in a way that is experiential, no longer values much the 'secondary benefits' it could have hoped for. What it wants from God, is God himself; nothing less than that can satisfy it. And hoping for God himself, is hoping, in faith, for an 'I don't know what', something beyond, a something that is always further out of reach.

The immensity of hope is founded on an immense poverty. For in the cruel light of this night we no longer count on anything but on God alone, and certainly not on ourselves, for our desire to be realised. Before, more or less, and without really being very aware of it, we counted on our religious habit and our 'correct' life, our virtue, our sacrifices, our prayers, and even on our humility! All that, insomuch as it was something coming from us, something 'pure', has been burnt up, and vanished.

Now we are standing naked and poor, stripped of all that made up our little person: the outward one we showed to others, to God too, and the inner person composed of our memories, emotions, and various acquisitions . . . our human journey of the past. All that is dead and buried. There now lives only a being who is born of the creative goodness of the Lord at each moment: a being who draws life uniquely from the forgiveness and merciful goodness of the Father. He counts on that alone. He knows that he deserves nothing, except for his sins. And yet he hopes, madly, beyond all reason, without doubting for one second, in God himself. For he, the Lord, is good. Eternal is his love.

THE NIGHT OF LOVE

If only we have love, we can endure anything. We can see this already on a human level; it is even more true with regard to God. But in the night, the soul loses all those feelings of love that it enjoyed before. Not only does it see itself as not loved by God, but as hated, persecuted, and pursued. And this is justice, for the soul is as sin in its own eyes. Because totally dissimilar to God, darkness, it sees itself as eternally separated from him, although, from afar, it continues to love him. The soul can draw no consolation from any creature, for the source of its ability to love and to enjoy seems to have dried up for good. The iron cauterizing its wounds enters into the heart and burns up all impurity. It is only after this, when the soul is healed, and totally poor, that it can receive the pure gratuity of Love: a Love that will give itself to the soul, and love in it.

23

Ecstatic Union

The Greek word 'ecstasy' means 'the action of being outside of oneself'. In ecstatic union the soul is completely withdrawn from corporal senses to be fixed unwaveringly on a supernatural object which attracts it and absorbs all its energy.

There are two essential elements:

(i)   The first, interior and invisible, is intense attention to a religious subject, and intimate communion with it.

(ii) The second, corporal and visible, is alienation of the senses.

It is the interior absorption that causes the alienation of the senses.

THE DIFFERENT KINDS OF ECSTASY

Ecstasy can be – natural: intellectual, artistic, pathological, chemical
                 – preternatural: diabolical
                 – supernatural: prophetic
                                  mystical

NATURAL ECSTASY

We can speak of natural ecstasy by analogy, when the soul is so absorbed in an object that it is more or less withdrawn from the material world: for example, the intellectual, concentrating on a sublime truth; the artist, lost in admiration in front of a beautiful work. There can also be states of exaltation provoked by extreme emotions (joy, anger, love) which for a while can absorb all other feelings.

The same alienation, but without its interior, positive content, can be induced by the action of drugs, by certain techniques of concentration, or by hypnosis; and we see it sometimes in trances of mediums, and in certain pathological conditions (catalepsy, etc.). In these cases there is a narrowing of the field of consciousness, or a deadening of the superior faculties, instead of the widening and intense activity of the intelligence that occurs in mystical ecstasy. Then there are the hallucinations seen in hospitals, and which consist always in fantasies of the imagination. They are visual, auditory or tactile, in contrast with the intellectual perceptions that we generally find in the ecstasies of the saints.

In short, the 'natural' ecstasy is infinitely inferior to that caused by divine action, although we can see a distant analogy in it. The action of God is always received in a human psychology.

DIABOLICAL ECSTASY

The devil can act on the imagination and sensibility of a person, and produce a state of ecstasy which, exteriorly, can look very much like genuine ecstasy. It will be seen for what it is by some note of impropriety about it, but chiefly by its fruits.

SUPERNATURAL PROPHETIC ECSTASY

There is an ecstasy caused by divine action when a message is being communicated to a prophet, and we can see many examples of this in the Bible.

SUPERNATURAL MYSTICAL ECSTASY

Three kinds:
1. Simple ecstasy, when it comes about gently and gradually, or if it is not very intense. Generally, in this case, it is supposed that it does not contain revelations.
2. Rapture, when the ecstasy is sudden and violent.
3. Flight of the spirit, when, as St Teresa tells us, 'it seems

that this impetuous rapture is in all truth tearing the spirit away from the body.'

Characteristics

At first, raptures cause great fear.

Usually, this violent movement cannot be resisted. In simple ecstasy, it is possible to resist, at least at the start.

The body stays in the attitude in which it has been surprised.

An expansion of the intelligence takes place, in which, nearly always, God reveals secrets of a supernatural order. Noble sights, profound ideas, come to the mind.

After a rapture, it is sometimes difficult for several days for the person to return to exterior occupations.

The person remembers what he has seen, but, more often than not, cannot express it in human language, and has to use images.

When returning from a rapture that has occurred in the middle of a conversation or a prayer, it often happens that the person continues the sentence that was interrupted, even after an interruption of several hours.

There is a wide variety of ages at which saints have become ecstatic, ranging from St Catherine of Siena, at the age of four, to St Teresa at the age of forty-three.

Duration: from half an hour, up to twelve hours or more.

Frequency: was very great in some saints, whose lives were a series of ecstasies. St Catherine of Siena had thousands of ecstasies.

The recall: the order of a legitimate superior or of a confessor brings the person in ecstasy back to his natural state, but nearly always with much suffering.

Corporal effects

Corporal insensitivity: there is no reaction to pricks, blows, etc.

However, the eyes of the person remain active and are fixed intently upon the divine vision; they appear to be enlarged; they do not see material objects. A hand can be passed in front of the eyes of an ecstatic without provoking any reaction.

Usually the person is immobile, but some walk about, or speak of their vision.

Natural warmth gradually diminishes, especially in the extremities – feet, hands.

The natural functioning of breathing, circulation, etc., is greatly slowed down.

Simple ecstasy rests the body (like sleep), whereas violent ecstasy tears and breaks it.

There is a luminous expression on the face of the ecstatic, reflecting the vision.

There is often levitation: the body rises above the ground, contrary to all the laws of nature.

Intellectual visions of God

In these raptures, God shows himself. The person has intellectual visions of divine things, of which the highest is the vision of the Holy Trinity.

Because of their very splendour, these visions are blinding for the human intelligence. This results in a mixture of light and darkness. As the communication intensifies, so the soul sinks deeper into the 'divine darkness'. This is particularly true of visions of those divine attributes which are 'un-shareable', and more incomprehensible for us: infinity, eternity, creative power, immutability, absolute being; and the absence of any real distinction between the attributes, and their fusion in one Good, undefinable and superior, and inclusive of all other good.

The attributes of beauty, justice, mercy, and intelligence are less obscure for us, we see analogies of them in creation.

Theologians insist on the fact that these visions are inferior to the beatific vision, in which God is seen as he is in himself, with no darkness; but it is already a very sublime, experiential knowledge of God. It is generally accorded that it is possible to enjoy, for a moment, the beatific vision properly speaking, but that this is an extremely rare grace.

Effects on the soul

In ecstatic union, there is an intimate union with God. It gives the soul a supernatural energy, the burning vitality of the Spirit, which inclines it to the heroic practice of all the Christian virtues. The ecstasy of love is always followed by the ecstasy of works. That is the surest touchstone of its authenticity.

So, above all, it is the personality and life of the saints which distinguishes them from others who are sick and disturbed. The saints are firm in spirit, their plans are vast and difficult to execute (St Teresa, St Ignatius, etc.). Their wills are full of energy and capable of fighting to overcome all kinds of opposition, and to obtain mastery over themselves. They have a very high moral ideal, and devote themselves to the glory of God and the good of their neighbour.

Graces freely given for the good of the Church

When this grace is given by God in view of some extraordinary task to be accomplished, it is often accompanied by a special charism of the Spirit: for example, utterance of wisdom, utterance of knowledge, gifts of an exceptionally strong faith, of healings, of miracles, of prophecies, the discernment of spirits, (the reading of hearts, sometimes), speaking in tongues, the interpretation of tongues, etc.

These are elevated and precious spiritual gifts, but let us never forget that the gift of love is infinitely superior to them, for God is Love.

> Strive for the greater gifts. And I will show you a still more excellent way. If I speak in the tongues of mortals and of angels, but do not have love, I am a noisy gong or a clanging cymbal. (1 Corinthians 12:31–13:1)

Why do ecstasies occur?

This may seem a strange question. But we have to ask it, because ecstasy, for as much as it alienates the senses and disturbs the psychic balance of life, has to be overcome, and will usually disappear in transforming union. So it is as yet an imperfect realisation of union with God, and it is precisely the exterior, spectacular side of it which reveals this imperfection. St John of the Cross tells us why:

Since, after all, the sensory part of the soul is weak and incapable of vigorous spiritual communications, these proficients, because of such communications experienced in the sensitive part, suffer many infirmities, injuries, and weaknesses of stomach, and as a result fatigue of spirit. As the Wise Man says: 'The corruptible body is a load upon the soul'. Consequently the communications imparted to proficients cannot be very strong, nor very intense, nor very spiritual – which is a requirement of the divine union – because of the weakness and corruption of the senses which have their share in them. Thus we have raptures and transports and the dislocation of bones, which always occur when the communications are not purely spiritual (communicated to the spirit alone) as are those of the perfect, who are already purified by the night of the spirit. For in the perfect, these raptures and bodily torments cease, and they enjoy freedom of spirit without a detriment to or transport of their senses.

This explains why the first spiritual graces can cause profound physical and psychic disturbances, as we see in many of the mystics. It is not easy for our poor human flesh to be transformed by the Spirit.

WHAT ABOUT OURSELVES?

We could praise God for the marvels he accomplishes in the saints, whilst being very far from all this ourselves. It has often been said: 'There are not many ecstatics at the Charterhouse'. The sobriety of the spiritual atmosphere here, and the discretion with regard to all exteriorisation of sentiments (exaggerated perhaps), is such, that the 'local ecstatic' would not feel very comfortable. And yet whatever the place and conventions may be, when this grace of the Spirit takes hold of a person, it is impossible for him to resist. So it looks as though the Lord gives this grace rarely here, at least in its exterior, spectacular form. Remember that it is a very elevated level of mystical life which, in any case, very few reach.

We saw too that, in themselves, ecstatic phenomena are a
transitional stage on the way towards the complete transparency
of transforming union. That is the aim: perfect conformity
with Christ in absolute docility to the Spirit, that is, to Love.
Insomuch as it is the normal fulfilment of the life of grace
in us, although rarely attained, it should be possible for this
transformation to be effected without the help of extraordinary
graces – more slowly perhaps, but no less surely. What other
meaning is there to our religious vows, our solitude, our silence,
our life of prayer and charity, if not that Christ should live fully
in us? Our whole life has to be ecstatic, a perpetual exit from
ourselves towards God and others. All love, if it is genuine, is
ecstatic. It is perhaps a good thing that in our desert this
'abrahamic' exit takes place in a humble, hidden way, incar-
nated in our simple, daily service and adoration, and spread
over the period of a lifetime. Let us be content with the treasure
of poverty in our journey of faith, and with the joy of pure
hope. May our death be the final ecstasy: our passover, our
passage to the Father.

24

Extraordinary Mystical Phenomena

These phenomena can accompany contemplation, without being an essential part of it.

They can be caused by:

- God: they are the effect of mystical union on the superior faculties and on the senses.
- Nature: produced by imagination, temperament, pathology.
- The devil.

Visions

Visions are perceptions of an object (any real object, a thing or a person) which by nature is invisible to a human being. They are:

- Sensory (apparitions): an objective reality is perceived by the senses (for example, the Virgin Mary).
- Imaginative: a picture of the object is produced in the imagination.
- Intellectual: a spiritual truth is perceived in a form inaccessible to the senses.

Words

These are communication of a thought, usually an affirmation, or a desire. They are:

- Auricular: perceived exteriorly through the ears.
- Imaginary: making themselves heard interiorly to the imagination.
- Intellectual: addressed directly to the intelligence.

Usually, visions and words go together.

Divine touches

There are also 'divine touches', spiritual sentiments imprinted in the will by a substance to substance contact of the soul with God. By essence, these belong to mystical union.

Revelations

A revelation is the manifestation of a hidden truth or of a secret, by a vision, a word, or a divine touch.

There are:

* Universal revelations, contained in the Bible or in the deposit of apostolic tradition, and transmitted by the Church. These came to an end with the preaching of the Apostles, and everyone must believe them.
* Particular or private revelations: made to individuals, without this universal, authenticated character. The Church does not oblige us to believe in them, even when, on rare occasions, she approves them. This approbation means that the revelations contain nothing which is contrary to the Scriptures and the doctrine of the Church. They can be proposed as probable and piously believable for our human faith. The value of these revelations is, neither more nor less, that of the testimony of the person who reports them.

Revelations of both kinds can be absolute, or under condition (for example, Jonas).

A supernatural revelation, given by God for the good of the soul of the person who receives it, has great efficacy. But there is great danger of illusion. An attitude of objectivity and prudent discernment are needed. This is especially true when the revelation is accompanied by a message destined to be spread or a mission to be accomplished (for example, to propagate a devotion or found a religious congregation).

BEWARE!

Everything to do with the senses and the imagination (visions, words and revelations) is subject to caution. There can be many sources of illusion: the devil, a desire for what is spectacular, an impressionable nature, a state of fatigue, certain mental illnesses. Intellectual words and visions, which are quite close to certain normal intellectual operations, can easily be taken for supernatural whereas they are only the products of our own mind. How many people have 'heard a voice that told me . . . '. The devil excels in mimicking divine action. The human mind that receives this action, if indeed it exists, easily interprets, embroiders, deforms, and augments.

It is fair to say too that women, who, we saw, are by nature in a position of advantage in the life of prayer (there are far more women than men who are mystics), are, in the same proportion, more subject to mystical illusion. Their nervous, delicate, affective temperament makes them more accessible to sentiment than to reason, and more disposed to passivity. When they love, they love more totally, body and soul. They give of themselves more generously. But they can also be inconstant, weak, insatiable for emotions, taking their desires for reality. It is not surprising that a piety in which feelings and imagination are predominant sometimes gives rise to spiritual illusions. The discernment here has to be particularly prudent.

RULES OF DISCERNMENT

(a) The person receiving the favour
Usually revelations are made to people who are not only fervent, but already raised to the mystical state; although God does sometimes make them to people of ordinary piety, and to sinners, often in order to convert them.

A distinction must be made between those whom God uses occasionally for an apparition or a revelation (for example, St Bernadette), and those for whom visions, words and revelations are an habitual part of their spiritual state. Great perfection must be expected of these latter. One should examine:

Their natural qualities:
Temperament: balanced or neurotic?
Mental state: common sense, and right judgement, or

exalted imagination, and excessive sensitivity; overall health or weakness?

Moral state: a calm or passionate person? usually
sincere and truthful, or deceitful?

Their supernatural qualities:
- solid, tested virtue, or sentiments of fervour?
- sincere humility, or a love of putting oneself forward,
  vanity (lack of humility is a very bad sign)?
- open and docile, or stubborn and impervious?
- whether or not there is passive purification and some
  degree of mystical prayer?

The presence of these qualities does not prove the existence of
a revelation, but makes the testimony of the visionary more
credible; their absence, without proving its non-existence,
makes it not very probable.

(b) The object of the revelations
Any revelation that is contrary to the faith or to accepted stan-
dards of good behaviour has to be rejected. Moreover, things
that are useless, simply curious, too prolix (in general), or
impossible to realise without a miracle, cannot be accepted as
the object of a revelation coming from God.

(c) The fruits
The action of God can at first produce a sentiment of fear or
astonishment; this will be followed by a lasting feeling of peace,
joy and security. The action of the devil, on the contrary,
causes joy at first, then distress, sadness and discouragement.

True revelations establish the soul in humility, obedience
and patience. False ones engender pride, presumption and
disobedience.

Sometimes, if something important is at stake, one can
humbly ask God for a sign of confirmation – but conditionally:
if it is his will, and really useful.

SOURCES OF ERROR

(a) Human activity mixed in with the supernatural action of
God, especially if the imagination and mind are particularly vivacious.

So it is that in private revelations we find errors of
the time regarding physical or historical knowledge. The
revelations of Catherine of Siena totally conform to Domi-
nican theology, and those of Maria d'Aguéda conform to
Franciscan theology.

(b) A divine revelation can be wrongly interpreted.

For example, St Vincent Ferrier had announced the
last judgement as near, and even seemed to confirm the
revelation by many miracles. Joan of Arc believed that she
would be rescued from being burnt at the stake.

(c) Alterations can be made unwittingly to a revelation, by
the visionary or by secretaries, in an effort to explain it.

ATTITUDES REGARDING PRIVATE REVELATIONS

We cannot do better than imitate the wise reserve of the Church
and the saints.* The Church proceeds slowly and prudently.
Before pronouncing herself, she requires convincing, cumu-
lative and convergent proof. And even then, in the case of a
favourable judgement, she does not oblige anyone to believe in
the revelation.

When the revelation involves carrying out some exterior task,
the pros and cons have to be considered carefully, in the light
of supernatural prudence. For the visionary, the surest rule is
to entrust to the Church (in the person of the confessor,
director or superior) the command received, and to follow
humbly the directions she gives.

---

*In *Les Grâces d'Oraison*, Père Poulain is of the opinion that 'it is not
imprudent to say that, in the case of people who have not reached a high
degree of sanctity, at least three-quarters of their revelations are illusions'
p. 337. In the revelations of canonised saints, he indicates many mistakes
and misrepresentations, as well as a mixture, often, of true and false
revelations.

The desire for visions and revelations is a great source of illusion in the spiritual life, and is strongly discouraged by the great mystics. Faith gives us a knowledge of God that is superior and purer. 'A light has risen in the darkness for the upright' (Psalm 111:4).

25
Psycho-physiological Phenomena

Levitation, light surrounding a person, mysterious fragrances, abstinence from food over long periods, bilocation, etc: these are the effects of spiritual grace, if indeed it is such, overflowing into the body and sensibility of the person. These phenomena can sometimes be seen in the absence of genuinely mystical grace. In themselves they are not supernatural, even though we are often unable to find an adequate scientific explanation for them. In any case, however spectacular they may be, they are of an order which differs completely from intimate union with God, the fruit of the theological virtues, accomplished experientially in mystical grace. When the cause is supernatural, they can be seen as an anticipation of the state the body is to have in the glory of the resurrection.

Depending on each case, the cause can be supernatural (God, the effect of mystical union, particularly in the period of ecstasy), preternatural (angels or demons), or natural (unknown para-psychic or physical forces: there is a grey area in this – it is difficult to distinguish the boundaries of what is 'natural').

The great mystics of all religions regard these phenomena, on the whole, as secondary and accidental. It would be a grave mistake to set them as the ultimate target of one's efforts. In this case they would become a serious obstacle to spiritual progress.

All these phenomena are to be found in many of the saints who were mystics, but also in people who were less holy, or not holy at all.

In any case, and particularly for us, whose vocation it is to be hidden in the heart of God, we must not run after the froth of spectacular, exterior manifestations, but seek the inner marrow of love, lived in the transparence of simplicity and in humility. The grace of Christ must, indeed, transfigure our whole being; but by giving us first a heart of flesh, that we may love in truth, and then a body which will in some way be transparent to the light of grace, the grace of the resurrection, grace of life and of joy.

26

Transforming Union

GRACE

My beloved is mine, and I am his. (Song of Songs 2:16)

Transforming union is the full development on earth of sanctifying grace, that is, the fulness of the life of Christ within us. Sadly, it is a state which is rarely reached, for it implies a plenitude of love. But, however far we may be from that state, we should know something about it, so as to be able to distinguish what is only transitory in the spiritual life, from that which pertains to its perfection.

There is one last trial, a testing of love, in which the soul, intensely drawn to the One it loves, aspires with its whole being to heavenly union. It is the desire to die, to break the chains of this life. If the Lord inspires this desire in the soul, it is in order to fulfil it, but in an unexpected way, by giving the grace of transforming union.

Sanctifying grace is the free gift of the alliance contracted by God with each one of us, in the Church. It consists in the gift of the Holy Spirit who communicates divine life to us: the knowledge and love which enable us to know and love God in an intimate exchange of personal friendship. He says to each of us, 'I am calling you and you are my friend'; and his creator Word establishes us in a sort of equality with him, of friend to friend (or, in other words, makes us share in the divine nature). The life of prayer is all about learning to live this friendship. We have to be gradually raised to this dignity, purified, and slowly transformed, until our will is one with the will of the Lord and our heart belongs totally to him. Love is at the heart of transforming union, it is the substance of it. The phenomena which usually manifest this state are secondary, and in some cases are quite hidden, or even absent.

The life of grace becomes conscious. God is experienced not only as the object of our acts of faith, hope and love, but as the interior source, the indwelling co-principle, of these acts. The sap of divine life flows in our faculties.

UNION

The term 'spiritual marriage' is sometimes used to indicate this fusion of two lives: an intimate and stable union, based on the total, mutual gift of love between two persons, a gift with implications of rights and duties. 'All that is mine is yours, and all that is yours is mine' (John 17:10).

The soul shares in the knowledge of God. It is given a mysterious knowledge, both luminous and obscure, by the love poured into it by the Holy Spirit. Love is itself a form of knowledge (St Gregory) that goes further than any knowledge that can be formulated in images or ideas. It plunges into the infinite reality of divine life. The Spirit is the flame of love in the soul, a brightly burning flame.

There is no longer any distance. God communicates himself to the soul by substantial touches, that is, directly, substance to substance, without passing by the faculties. Plunged into the divine fire, the soul becomes fire. Immersed in the vast sea, the drop of water becomes sea. Traversed by light, the pane of glass becomes light, without however ceasing to be what it is. No image can adequately express the reality. The saints and great mystics of all times have tried to speak of it, but this irruption of infinite life into the tiny space of a human soul is beyond words; do we not however, each one of us, recognise in this, in some obscure way, our deepest desire? How strange. But not so strange really, for our heart is made for you, Lord.

This union is the source of special insights on God and on the mysteries of the faith: sparks from the furnace at the centre, that the intelligence receives by way of intuitive knowledge. The faculties no longer operate in their usual way, which is more or less discursive, but in the mode of the Holy Spirit acting through the gifts of intelligence and wisdom.

THE DWELLING OF THE HOLY TRINITY

In this state, there is an habitual vision of the presence of God in the centre of the soul, which is perceived, without mediation, as the dwelling of God. The higher faculties are drawn passively and imperiously towards the deep centre of the soul where God dwells. They are plunged into this source of life, and emerge from it transformed, to act at the exterior. The activity of the soul flows from this deep centre, the initiative comes from the interior and not from outside, from the Spirit and not from the world. This is why it is so important for the person of prayer to be able to enter into the interior depths of his or her soul, to remain there habitually, and to act from that centre.

The soul often possesses habitually, but with differing degrees of intensity, the vision of the Holy Trinity, or of the divine nature. This is the highest point of spiritual illumination, but paradoxically is sometimes called 'the Great Darkness',* for in drawing nearer, God reveals himself to be supreme mystery, and totally different.

Whether this vision concerns the divine persons or their unique nature, seems to depend on the religious sensitivity of the soul and the path followed. There is an Eastern tradition particularly directed towards experience of the divine nature, without however excluding, or regarding as secondary, loving intimacy with the persons of the Holy Trinity. But at this level of mystical experience, however necessary the concepts of nature and person may be, they are very inadequate with regard to the incandescent reality of the union of God.

---

*'If someone sees God, and understands what he sees, it is not God that he has contemplated, but one of the things that come from God, and that we are able to understand' (Denys the Mystic).

BY THE SPIRIT

The Holy Spirit is in charge of the whole of this transformation. It is the Spirit who acts in us as the principle of our sanctification. He inclines the soul to these supernatural acts, not by passing through the faculties, from outside, but from inside, from his dwelling in the centre, in the substance of the soul. Thus the Spirit moves the faculties, but in his own particular way, enabling them to attain their objects directly with an assurance and strength beyond their normal possibilities. Paradoxically, there is great liberty in this, for the soul is not moved like a lifeless puppet, but as someone who is free. This is a great mystery. The spiritual acts flow freely from a person transformed in his very substance by the Spirit; and these acts express perfectly the most intimate depths of that person, there where he adheres to God so closely that, with God, he is spirit, and source of life (1 Corinthians 6:17).

It is easy to say words that mean nothing, or say too much. It has been suggested – and by the mystics sometimes – that the soul breathes the Spirit with the Father and the Son; that it creates the world; that, placed within God's creative act, it is maintaining all things; that, in a game of love, it gives God to God, since God has in all truth given himself to the soul . . . All this is true, but in a sense that in no way diminishes the infinite transcendence of the Lord which is radically beyond our grasp. What is clear is that, by grace, in transforming union, the soul is plunged into a life that is infinitely beyond anything that we can possibly imagine. The fine shell of its little personality becomes perfectly transparent to the marvellous light in which it bathes. The soul is known and it knows. It is loved and it loves: perfectly, beyond anything we can possibly imagine or hope for.

TRANSFORMED INTO CHRIST

And all of us, with unveiled faces, seeing the glory of the Lord as though reflected in a mirror, are being transformed into the same image from one degree of glory to another; for this comes from the Lord, the Spirit. (2 Corinthians 3:18)

We set off to seek God, following in the steps of Jesus, on the path of the beatitudes of poverty and purity of heart, by the way of the cross and of love, towards the Father. Now at the end, we find Christ again, but the risen Christ. The extraordinary phenomena of the mystical life are an irruption in our world of the life of the resurrection, rays of light from Mount Tabor. If we can come to the Father in all confidence, as sons, it is because of the grace of Christ communicated to us through the Spirit. We are taken up into the life of Christ, we become as it were one person with him, to constitute what Augustine called 'the total Christ'. 'It is no longer I who live, but it is Christ who lives in me' (Galatians 2:20).

When the Word became flesh, he did not eliminate human nature, but raised it, rather, to the fulness of its liberty and perfection; and in the same way, when divine life takes flesh, so to speak, in us – not hypostatically, but by union of grace – our humanity is not eliminated, but radically transformed. It really is our own self that is transformed; myself, with my own features, my character, my feelings, my personal history, my wounds, my limits, my sufferings, my sensitivity . . . Christ in his glory bears the marks of the nails. The glory he communicates to us is the glory of humanity redeemed, and is all the more luminous because of that. The bread that we offer to be consecrated is the bread of our whole nature. That is why the Eucharist is so important: for there, the body and blood of Christ, the living humanity of Christ, touches us, penetrates us, in order to transform us into himself.

The spiritual person does not become an angel, he or she becomes Christ. And just as so few were able to recognise God in Jesus, so we too often pass by the saints. We look out for the extraordinary and the spectacular, and all we find is something marvellously human, a humanity that is in the likeness of God.

Generally there are not many extraordinary sensory

phenomena, and hardly any more ecstasies.* The human nature of the mystic is now used to God's action, and has adapted to it. On the level of the senses, there is no resistance, and the higher faculties have been strengthened in their usual mode of activity.

We are so concerned with the outward show of sanctity, with appearances! Yet the whole life of a monk, and especially of the solitary monk, is on the level of being, where all show is ridiculous comedy. The 'little' Theresa said once: 'There is no need for appearances, as long as the reality is there. Our Lord died of love on the cross, and yet look at his agony.'

And all is humility, because humility is born of truth. In this ultimate intimacy with the Lord, the monk knows, he experiences, that all is grace, that all comes from God. He takes stock of his own minute little self in the shadow of the greatness of God, the greatness of infinite Love. He makes no effort to be humble. We do not need light to see daylight.

In the mystic, the struggle between attention to God and contact with the world no longer exists. Throughout the whole development of the life of prayer, we have seen a ligature of the powers of the soul, from the partial withdrawal from the world in the prayer of quietude, up to the point of ecstasy, when all its usual activity in relation to the surrounding world becomes impossible: it has to be Martha or Mary. But from now on, we find Martha and Mary living together in harmony. Interior union with God is not hindered by the activity of Martha, and vice versa.

There are two levels of conscience, simultaneously occupied each with its own object, natural or supernatural, without hampering one another. This is the secret of the activity of the great saints, which is so fruitful spiritually: it flows from the source, without leaving it. Everything in the saints is unity, and they have tremendous strength to act – if God calls them to do so – and to suffer.

---

*Some saints always remain subject to ecstasies. It is perhaps a matter of temperament or of special grace.

The soul is not exempt from temptations and trials, which are usually of short duration; but it is not deeply affected by them. The great peace in the depths of the heart is not troubled, even when the surface is tossed by the storm. 'My peace I leave with you' (John 14:27).

Let us not forget that, except for a few moments on Mount Tabor, Christ offered us the humble, hidden image of the Servant. He renounced, precisely, the outward show of glory that so attracts our ambivalent desires. The light of a soul transformed by grace often dwells in a humanity which seems quite ordinary, sometimes even in one that is heavily burdened, always in one that is simple. Christian perfection does not lie in the Greek ideal of an earthly fulfilment of all one's human potential; its aim is the plenitude of charity, which, in a world marked by sin, can take the form of sacrifice and suffering assumed in a consent of faith, and of which the fulfilment is on the other side of death, in eternal life.

> See what love the Father has given us,
> that we should be called the children of God;
> and that is what we are! . . .
> Beloved, we are God's children now;
> what we will be has not yet been revealed.
> What we do know is this:
> when he is revealed, we will be like him,
> for we will see him as he is.
>
> (1 John 3:1, 2)

Maranatha!

CPSIA information can be obtained at www.ICGtesting.com
Printed in the USA
LVOW060023040512

280308LV00001B/178/A